T029146l

Museum Store

MUSEUM STORE ASSOCIATION

Established in 1955, the Museum Store Association is a nonprofit, international association organized to advance the success of nonprofit retail and of the professionals engaged in it. By encouraging high standards of professional competence and conduct, MSA helps nonprofit retail professionals at museums and cultural institutions better serve their organizations and the public. MSA supports museum stores and vendor affiliates through publications, annual meetings, regional chapters, networking, and professional resources.

Titles available from the Museum Store Association:

The New Store Workbook, third edition, revised with new content in 2015 by Susan DeLand, DeLand Consulting, Long Beach, California

Museum Store: The Manager's Guide, fourth edition, revised with new content in 2015 by Susan DeLand, DeLand Consulting, Long Beach, California

Museum Store Association Retail Industry Report, 2022 edition

Marketing Cultural and Heritage Tourism by Rosemary Rice McCormick

Museum Store
The Manager's Guide
Basic Guidelines for the New Museum Store Manager

Fifth Edition

Museum Store Association

MUSEUM STORE ASSOCIATION

ROWMAN & LITTLEFIELD
Lanham • Boulder • New York • London

Museum Store Association
PO Box 3861
Greenwood Village, CO 80155
www.museumstoreassociation.org

Published by Rowman & Littlefield
An imprint of The Rowman & Littlefield Publishing Group, Inc.
4501 Forbes Boulevard, Suite 200, Lanham, Maryland 20706
www.rowman.com

86-90 Paul Street, London EC2A 4NE

Copyright © 2024 by The Rowman & Littlefield Publishing Group, Inc.

Contributing Editors:
Melody Caban, Founder, Melody Cabán Consulting
Elizabeth Price, Executive Director, Museum Store Association
Kate Botelho Sibya, Retail Operations Manager, The Preservation Society of Newport County/
Newport Mansions
Julie Steiner, Senior Director of Admissions and Retail Operations, The Barnes Foundation
Susan Tudor, Director of Retail and Visitor Experience, Cummer Museum
Karen McNeely, Director of Retail Operations, Milwaukee Art Museum

Notice: Product or corporate names may be trademarks or registered trademarks and are used
only for identification and explanation without intent to infringe.

British Library Cataloguing in Publication Information Available

Library of Congress Cataloging-in-Publication Data
Names: Museum Store Association (U.S.)
Title: Museum store : the manager's guide : basic guidelines for the new
  museum store manager / Museum Store Association.
Description: Fifth edition. | Lanham : Rowman & Littlefield Publishers,
  [2024] | Includes bibliographical references and index.
Identifiers: LCCN 2024015471 (print) | LCCN 2024015472 (ebook) | ISBN
  9781538185315 (cloth ; alk. paper) | ISBN 9781538185322 (paperback ;
  alk. paper) | ISBN 9781538185339 (epub)
Subjects: LCSH: Museum stores—Management. | Merchandising.
Classification: LCC HF5469.65 .M8697 2024 (print) | LCC HF5469.65 (ebook)
  | DDC 658.8/7—dc23/eng/20240405
LC record available at https://lccn.loc.gov/2024015471
LC ebook record available at https://lccn.loc.gov/2024015472

∞™ The paper used in this publication meets the minimum requirements of American National
Standard for Information Sciences—Permanence of Paper for Printed Library Materials, ANSI/
NISO Z39.48-1992.

Contents

Preface

The revised and updated fifth edition of *Museum Store: The Manager's Guide* includes invaluable new tools not available in previous editions. Look for

- store marketing using modern technologies and communication channels;
- updated information on diversity, equity, access, and inclusion (DEAI) and its role in museum store operations;
- how-tos for analyzing and measuring financial performance, visual merchandising, choosing a POS system, managing personnel, and more; and
- *bonus*: forms found in the book that you can download from the MSA website.

This practical guide is a "must own" resource for every nonprofit retail professional. The eight-chapter volume includes a wealth of advice on best practices compiled by the MSA to help professionals become more successful in every aspect of their business. Get guidance from experience store manager pros to help you correctly evaluate your store's performance and get on track to boost every aspect of performance. If you add just one educational resource to your library this year, this book should be it! The information it contains is *that* valuable.

1

The Retail Store

AN INTEGRAL PART OF THE MUSEUM

Chapter Highlights

- The role of the museum store: nonprofit retail
- The store as an educational resource
- Writing a mission statement
- Following best practices for an ethical museum store
- Beyond profitability: winning a seat at the table

The museum store concept has successfully become one of the most exciting areas in retail. The quality of merchandise, the educational aspect of the products, and the link to the total museum experience all contribute to the sustained appeal of museum stores for the general public. From art museums to historical sites, children's museums to nature centers, and everything in between, the popularity of museum stores remains high for all types of cultural organizations.

Recognizing the growing need for museums to generate earned income, museum leaders are now giving greater attention to their retail operations than ever before. The recognition of the importance of museum store operations is accompanied by a heightened level of expertise and sophistication in the field of museum store management. Together these factors have made museum stores a crucial segment in retail.

THE ROLE OF THE MUSEUM STORE: NONPROFIT RETAIL

With economic constraints propelling museum stores to be more professional, entrepreneurial, and creative, confusion can emerge regarding the idea of retail in a not-for-profit setting. The term "nonprofit retail" does not refer to unprofitable operations; rather, it means that the overall purpose of the retail operation is to benefit the nonprofit parent entity. This is not a violation of a museum's nonprofit status; in fact, museum store managers are committed to running profitable operations to further the museum's nonprofit purpose.

The museum store strives to offer products that reflect the purpose and quality of their institution. This is the single most important factor separating nonprofit retail from a strictly commercial operation.

Successful store managers keep the museum's mission in mind in all aspects of their work: when buying and producing merchandise, training staff, and displaying products. By doing this, they gain the respect and collaboration of other cultural professionals while building a dedicated customer base.

Nonprofit retail in the museum setting is unique, exciting, and challenging, as is the role of the store manager. The store serves the museum by supporting the museum's brand and voice, extending the visitor's educational experience, and providing an additional revenue source. It also serves the visitor who wants to take home a tangible connection to the museum experience and usually visits the store as a last stop before leaving. This gives the store, through display, product mix, and customer interaction with staff, an opportunity to make this last impression a great one. This should echo the visitors' interaction with the exhibitions and extend their impressions in a powerful and positive way.

THE STORE AS AN EDUCATIONAL RESOURCE

The store must be viewed as an educational extension of the museum that reflects its collections, exhibitions, and programs. This is just as important as its financial role in supporting the institution. The store manager's responsibility is to see that key museum administrators understand the store's educational function and support the store accordingly.

Store managers must champion the store's role as an integral part of the museum's educational and earned revenue function to museum administrators. There can be tension between the store manager and other museum professionals, who may see the store only as a commercial entity rather than an academic or mission-based part of the institution. Unless an organization makes persistent efforts to mitigate this tension, one could spend more time working through political snares than on store operations. Avoid these perceptions by making informed and focused choices regarding the books and products sold.

Seek to collaborate with other members of the museum staff for the greater mission of the institution. Ask the advice of the curators, educators, marketing staff, and other stakeholders on sensitive merchandise decisions. Strong working relationships with staff across the organization can have great results. Consider convening a retail advisory group to gain support across departments while ensuring retail operations are integrated with other mission-directed museum initiatives.

Because the store serves as a reflection of the museum, think carefully about the image you want to project and select merchandise accordingly. Ask yourself what niche your store can fill. Perhaps it's the best art bookstore in the city or the best source for local crafts. Work with your marketing and communications teams to excel in the area in which you choose to concentrate, and make sure your brand story is aligned with your institutional identity.

When selecting merchandise, constantly ask, "How does this relate to my museum?" If the connection is shaky, resist buying. The second question to ask is, "Can I sell it?" If so, you're on the right track. Review the merchandise on a regular basis, and reevaluate how it relates to the museum's collections, exhibitions, and programs. Staying close to your organization's mission will be your guide as you and your financial officer decide whether or not unrelated business income tax (UBIT) will be due on sales.

WRITING A MISSION STATEMENT

A mission statement is a tool to keep you and others informed of and focused on the purpose of the museum store. If it seems the store is getting away from its original intent because of changing circumstances or the busy pace of retail, refer to the mission statement. If no statement is in place, write one and put it into effect. Use it for yourself and share it with staff, the museum, and the community to communicate the store's purpose. A mission statement involves several key steps:

- Refer to the museum's statement of purpose as stated in the nonprofit tax documents.
- Compose a simple, short, clear store mission that reflects the museum's statement of purpose and the institutional mission statement.
- Get approval for the store mission statement from the museum administration.

Here are some sample mission statements:

- The purpose of the Photography Museum Store is to further the educational goals of the Photography Museum by providing visitors with merchandise for purchase that is related to the museum collections and exhibits and by providing earned income to the museum through profits on sales in the store.
- The Natural History Museum Store extends the educational experience of the museum to its visitors and provides financial support to the operations of the Natural History Museum.
- The Botanical Garden Store's mission is to offer horticulture and botanical products and information for sale to the garden's visitors. The store will

provide education and delight to the visitor and funding to the garden's programs through earned revenue.

Merchandise policies then follow logically from the mission statement. Keep in mind that issues concerning ethics, the mission statement, and UBIT are all related.

FOLLOWING BEST PRACTICES FOR AN ETHICAL MUSEUM STORE

PERSONNEL

In issues of personnel, it is the responsibility of museum store management to follow good employment practices because the public perception of the museum store is closely tied to the parent institution. They must recruit, train, and support staff at a high level of professionalism and make the working environment safe, inclusive, and supportive of employees with diverse backgrounds, perspectives, and skills.

Similarly, it is the responsibility of museum store staff to be knowledgeable about the collections and mission of the organization and to be fully aware of the source, quality, authenticity, and educational worth of all items sold in the store. Misrepresentations, whether intentional or not, reflect upon the reputation of the museum as well as the museum store. All museum store personnel, whether paid or volunteer, are representatives of the museum.

Volunteer managers are ethically obligated to ensure that their volunteer status is not used as an excuse to exploit the commercial role of the museum store at the expense of its educational function. It is unethical for museum store personnel to use their museum affiliation for personal profit or to engage in any activity that may compromise the integrity of the institution or undermine the confidence of the museum staff and the public.

PRODUCTS

As designated sites of cultural significance, preserving and presenting valued collections held in the public trust, museums owe it to their communities to uphold the strongest standards of ethical practices. This duty extends to the museum's stores, and store managers should stay educated about best practices across a range of topics: diversity, equity, accessibility, and inclusion (DEAI) initiatives; merchandise practices; employment law; financial accounting; and data security, among others. This handbook presents the current industry best practices for many of these important areas in the following chapters. Museums are a pride of their communities and serve as pillars and destinations. The museum store manager, then, has an opportunity to present a business enterprise that epitomizes the community's ideals in a practical, pragmatic way. With that community trust in mind, it is to a museum store manager's advantage to maintain the highest standards in all areas.

Museum stores have an obligation to follow all local, state, and federal laws and museum industry ethics standards concerning the sale of antiquities; archaeological artifacts; products from endangered species, plants, and wildlife; or other commercially restricted items. Keep informed of the laws in your location. If relevant, consult with your museum's curators and director to set guidelines and policies for presenting and selling Native American ethnological materials in your institution.

Stay active and informed on museum policies regarding different kinds of merchandise, such as ivory, mineral specimens, animal byproducts, and architectural artifacts. The Museum Store Association (MSA) has adopted ethics policies to serve as guidelines on these matters, and they re available on the website: www.museumstoreassociation.org.

Policies regarding the propriety of manufacturing reproductions, replicas, and derived products vary from museum to museum. Their sale in museum stores must be clearly communicated so that they are not misconstrued by the public. All reproductions and replicas must be identified as such.

Museum store managers are also obligated to learn and observe applicable copyright laws. Advertising implying that reproductions are original works is unethical, misleading, and in some instances illegal. Any representation suggesting that the value of a reproduction appreciates is also unacceptable.

The sale of any deaccessioned museum collection items through the museum store is unethical. Even though the item may have been officially deaccessioned, the public may perceive the transaction as the museum store participating in the liquidation of the museum's collection.

TECHNOLOGY

Ethics also extends to museum store websites, which are an extension of the museum and subject to the organization's information and fair use policies. Museum stores have an ethical responsibility to post in an easy-to-find and clearly written manner a policy detailing how they collect, track, use, and disclose information gathered about website visitors. Visitors to museum store websites should be assured that information collected for one purpose is not shared or sold to a third party without their consent. Visitors should also be assured that by providing personal information they will not receive unwanted solicitations.

BEYOND PROFITABILITY: WINNING A SEAT AT THE TABLE

Understanding the museum store's role in the museum, building a merchandise presentation with the museum's educational mission in mind, developing a strong mission statement, forming robust collaborations with other museum departments, and implementing key ethical practices in all operations goes a long way toward creating a store that is a valuable destination for museum visitors.

Admittedly, retail is a business, and business has a cost associated with it. For many museums, following the practices outlined in the following chapters of this handbook for buying, merchandising, display, financial assessment, and marketing will result in a store that also contributes meaningful earned revenue to the museum's bottom line.

Although large-scale museums are often the first to come to mind when thinking about the industry, the fact is that most museums are quite small: historic sites and houses, gardens, libraries, small art collections, museums affiliated with schools or municipalities, and so many other museums may not see the volume of visitors required to support a financially robust business operation.

The Museum Store Retail Industry Report shares that 25 percent of museum stores gross less than $90,000 in annual sales. Running a profitable store at that scale is, in many cases, simply not possible. Larger businesses benefit from economies of scale in purchasing, business systems, staffing costs, and other operational factors that simply may be out of reach to smaller museums.

Data aggregated from across industry reports shows that museums with stores with less than $300,000 in annual sales often run merely breaking even or at a small loss, especially when using paid personnel rather than volunteers. In these instances, the museum store serves as a visitor amenity. The museum makes a choice to provide a retail store often as a marketing tool to support educational initiatives and extend visitors' engagement with the museum. The museum store manager's business focus changes from profit to minimizing losses and working as close to that breakeven point as possible.

For museum stores in this situation, it's particularly important to understand the store's value proposition beyond profits. *The Manager's Guide* is invaluable for managers in their overall job of advocating for their store even if it is not financially profitable for the museum because it equips them with comprehensive insights and strategies to effectively communicate the broader benefits of the store. Beyond just revenue generation, the guide underscores the store's role in enhancing visitor experiences, supporting the museum's mission, and fostering community engagement. This resource empowers managers to make a compelling case for the store's integral role in the museum's overall success, illustrating its value in terms of branding, educational impact, and audience connection, which can be essential for securing ongoing support and recognition within the institution, irrespective of its financial performance.

Overall, museum stores provide a unique proposition: uniting the lofty educational mission of a museum with the familiar and comforting environment of a commercial enterprise, fulfilling the chance to both educate and generate revenue all at once. As a result, managing a museum store can be a tightrope walk, balancing opposing needs, weighing money and mission in a delicate balance. But it is this balance that ultimately gives museum stores the reputation of being exceptional places to shop, find unique gifts, and support meaningful causes.

SUMMARY POINTS

- The museum store's products should reflect the purpose and quality of the parent institution.
- A mission statement helps keep you focused on the purpose of the store.
- Clear ethics policies help museum stores achieve their mission with integrity.

2

Building Budgets and Tracking Stats

- Formulating a budget
- Budget projections
- Cash flow
- Measuring sales performance
- Metrics versus mission
- Establishing accounting procedures and maintaining accurate records
- Building organizational mission and DEAI priorities into your store's budget

Effective retail businesses, be they nonprofit or for-profit, are defined by skilled management teams that implement a reliable and comprehensive system of allocating, tracking, and controlling money. Responsible management of your store's funds encompasses everything from formulating a budget and forecasting projections to keeping necessary records.

It is best to use a software point-of-sale (POS) system with inventory and accounting controls to develop these tools (further discussed in chapter 3). Work with your accounting department to ensure your software reports complement their analysis and recordkeeping.

FORMULATING A BUDGET

Think of a budget as a dynamic framework operating within approved parameters. When used inflexibly, budgets can stifle a store's potential. Be cautious of living too stringently by your budget. Don't jeopardize your store's well-being simply because a line item in the budget won't permit a necessary expense. On the other hand, exercise caution if straying too far from budget guidelines.

Your budget should be written as a monthly projection, following your museum store's fiscal year (January–December, July–June, and October–September are common for museums). Your budget also clearly sets out a museum's mission-driven initiatives and establishes priorities and specifications for any project with costs associated that can result in costs for the retail store.

Budgets can be a valuable tool for managers. When used wisely, they provide a blueprint for sound fiscal policies. Carefully prepared budgets allow management to compare projections with results, make the most profitable use of a store's funds, and monitor internal functions.

BUDGET DEVELOPMENT

Before preparing your annual operating budget, you'll need to study last year's budget and income statement (also called a profit-and-loss [P&L] statement). To gauge whether there will be an increase or decrease in overall growth, consult with your chief operating officer or accounting director to assess your institution's anticipated business budget. This approach guarantees alignment between your store's performance and your institution's budget forecasts. If previous figures are not available, generate figures based on industry percentages and by talking with other museum store managers and specialty retailers in your region. The Museum Store Association Retail Industry Report, 2022 edition, is the best resource for you to validate or create budget assumptions for your store.

Make sure you have the following figures at your fingertips:

- Historical average transaction
- Historical net sales
- Historical cost of goods sold
- Historical sales
- Projected visitation
- Projected per capita spending

With that done, you are ready to determine the working numbers for your operating budget. These include the following:

- Estimated retail sales
- Target gross profit margin
- Estimated direct expenses

BUDGET PROJECTIONS

RETAIL SALES

To determine estimated retail sales, take your visitation pro ction and compare it with the previous period. Then apply the percentage (fference to your historical retail sales numbers to establish your initial benchr ark projection.

Next evaluate your expectations for the coming year. he store's past performance coupled with institutional knowledge can he determine the appropriate percentage increase or decrease. Many cultural stores are at the mercy of their organization's exhibition schedule, programmi , and visitation. Work with the respective departments as they prepare thei own budgets to gain information about timing, any restrictions, and attendance projections. Also include your communications and marketing departments. Knowing how much money they are allocating to an exhibition or program telegraphs their attendance expectation, which translates to your sales per visitor.

Collectively, this knowledge can inform your sales projections. Another source to inform your sales projections is historical records of past exhibitions. If your museum had an exhibition on Impressionist art during the summer months, you are likely to see extremely good sales figures. If it had an exhibition on obscure sculpture, you may see weaker sales. If there was severe weather that forced road closures, this will be reflected in the sales figures. Be an anthropologist. Record and study your store history. Base your spending on a realistic assessment of future income. By using a monthly budget, you can more accurately manage the timing of revenues and expenses as they fall in with your institution's calendar and larger institutional influences on your business.

- If you expect a better year, take last year's sales figure and add an informed percentage.
- If you expect a decline in sales, take last year's sales figure and subtract an appropriate percentage.
- Identify the fixed costs versus the costs that will fluctuate with revenue changes.
- Identify any new projects or initiatives that mean new expenses in the year to come.

TARGET GROSS PROFIT MARGIN

Next you need to determine the cost of goods sold by establishing a target gross profit margin (GPM):

$$\text{Gross Profit Margin (\%)} = \text{Gross Profit} \div \text{Gross Sales}$$

Product categories have different margins. Because the publishing industry controls much of the retail pricing on books, stationery, and paper goods, the wholesale discounts are often subject to quantity discount schedules, and profit margins on these items tend to be slim. This is not problematic if you can make a merchandise plan that compensates by buying and selling other products with higher profit margins. Jewelry traditionally can be sold at a higher markup. Certain gift items support a higher retail price. Proprietary products often have the highest margin of all. Your expenses help you to determine your average GPM because all expenses are subtracted from the gross profit to produce your bottom line or net profit. This is an extremely important contribution to your institution's budget. A general rule could be to target an average GPM of 56 percent or higher.

ESTIMATED DIRECT EXPENSES

When you increase sales and allocate funds for direct expenses, think carefully before providing an automatic funding increase. Budgets that grow by precedent and fixed percentage rather than by real need can become inefficient and unwieldy. The following are sample questions to answer to determine how much or little your revenue will increase or decrease and in what months changes will happen. In this instance, rules that apply to for-profit retail may not apply to a store in a cultural organization.

Evaluate the commercial potential for each of the following:

- Will planned exhibitions or events draw an increase in visitation?
- Does the subject matter lend itself to product development?
- Is there related product available from other like organizations or from the trade?
- What time of year will the exhibition be held? Is it a high-potential shopping period such as during the winter holidays?
- Ask your marketing department (or equivalent) what percentage of its budget it is putting toward each exhibition or program. If it is not advertising, it may not think there is potential for audience draw and is saving its money to promote a more important exhibition.
- Will your organization be dark during high-visitation periods such as summer or spring and winter breaks?
- Do you have patterns in your visitation and sales history that support seasonal increases?
- Were there any events that changed your revenues significantly in previous years?
- Will they be repeated?
- Were they out of your control?

Here are some questions to ask when projecting expenses:

- Will some exhibitions or events necessitate hiring more staff?

- Will they be temporary, full time, or part time?
- In which month(s) will you hire?
- Will you need to update or increase display fixtures?
- Will increased revenues require that you purchase more packaging and office supplies?
- Will there be rate increases from carriers (USPS, FedEx, UPS, Yellow Freight, etc.)?
- Will postage increase?
- Will the cost of paper increase for printing posters, postcards, etc.?
- Check on aging equipment: Will you have to replace or upgrade?
- Think about your existing software platforms: Will they be sufficient to support your business in the year ahead, or will you be adding new options?
- Will there be additional travel required?
- Can you renegotiate your bank charges? With the increased popularity of online marketplaces, can you expect an increase in credit card fees or bank charges?

Organizations charge their stores' expenses differently. It is common to have the general operation budget expense mortgage or rent costs, utilities, facilities, and security. By doing this, it simplifies the budgeting process for all. A successfully operated store contributes to the general operating line with its net profit.

Visit the MSA website to download a sample comparative budget template available in the MSA Resource Library. This sample template lists likely expenses for a store, but you can customize it for your own use. Extend the template to include months and budget for the entire year. To read and analyze your financials easily and efficiently, it is a best practice to group expenses into categories. An example is salary-related expenses. Cultural stores tend to have more frontline staff than for-profit stores to be able to ensure the best possible customer experience. As a rule of thumb, staff salary-related costs are about 25 percent to 30 percent of total sales. List state and federal payroll taxes and benefits as separate lines and subtotal to see the impact of staffing on your revenue.

CASH FLOW

Note: This analysis is only relevant to stores that keep a separate bank account from the rest of their organization.

Once you've formulated a budget, you'll need to decide when to spend your money. If you don't have extensive records to study, the simplest method for determining expenditures is to divide the estimated cost of goods by twelve to give you a monthly purchasing figure or by four to give you a quarterly or seasonal purchasing figure. However, purchasing money need not be distributed evenly. If your store has a history of uneven seasonal performance—holiday sales greatly outpace summer sales or vice versa, sales tied to exhibitions and events—you will want to distribute the money accordingly.

A method for allocating money involves preparing a twelve-month cash flow statement. This tells you how much available cash you have at a given point in time. Compiling a cash flow statement simply involves tracking sales and expenditures:

- First determine the monthly cash inflow (sales figures for each month of the fiscal year).
- Then determine the monthly cash outflow. Break down inventory purchases and direct expenses. Remember, in cash flow, inventory purchases are based on when you pay the invoice, not when you order or receive the merchandise. If you can negotiate extended payment terms, you can pay the bill with some of the money from the sale of the goods.
- Subtract monthly cash outflow (disbursements) from cash inflow to arrive at monthly cash excess or, as the case may be, deficit.
- Add monthly cash excess or deficit to the cash available to the store at the beginning of the month.

The total tells you how much cash the store will have at the end of the month.

When developing the merchandise plan for the coming year's purchases and expenditures, study the cash flow statement for peaks and valleys.

- Were inventory purchases especially high during a particular season?
- Did display expenses increase with exhibitions?
- Were supply costs higher during the holidays?
- Did you add extra staff?

If you expect the coming year to repeat the prior year's patterns, simply plug in last year's numbers rounded up to the nearest $100. If you anticipate changes, adjust accordingly. Be sure to factor in any expenses or revenue changes that might be expected with special exhibitions.

MEASURING SALES PERFORMANCE

By monitoring key performance indicators (KPIs), you can gauge how seasonal patterns, special exhibitions, etc. affect sales traffic. Analysis of this data enables you to plan special incentives, such as sales and advertising campaigns, for traditionally slow periods. You can also use the data to evaluate your strengths and weaknesses. For example, if your sales-per-visitor figures are low, perhaps you want to enhance your personalized customer service. You may also want to look at the visibility of the store and be sure that all visitors see it and have the option of shopping.

Ratios, or metrics, present the relationship of one thing to another. Because ratios provide a mechanism for measuring and comparing, they are essential for evaluating a store's operations. To make ratios meaningful, you need to track them from month to month and year to year. Compare them not only against each other but with figures from other stores. The MSA Retail Industry Report, 2022 edition (available at www.museumstoreassociation.org), provides some of the most current information about other stores by gross sales and type.

To determine ratios, stores must have a method to capture and track sales. Ideally, this is a POS system, but if the store does not have such a system, then the store manager needs to devise a system.

Building a metric dashboard for your store is a highly successful way of monitoring financial health. Just as you check the dashboard in your car before you drive, you want your business to be properly fueled and running smoothly. It is better to make adjustments daily or weekly than to find out you didn't make your projection. A budget is a planning tool, but it doesn't necessarily give insight into how success or failure is happening. The following are some benchmarks that can guide you to make nimble adjustments.

METRICS TO WATCH

Gross margin return on inventory investment (GMROII): For a nonprofit store whose budget is a part of the larger institutional budget, gross margin return on inventory investment may be a more accurate and useful tool than a statement of cash flow. Performing GMROII analysis keeps you tuned to how well your inventory investment is working. A high GMROII indicates a good balance of sales, margins, and inventory cost. This may be calculated monthly and annually.

GMROII (gross margin return on inventory investment)=
Gross Margin% ÷ Average Inventory at Cost

Average Inventory at Cost = BOM (beginning of month) Inventory
at Cost + EOM (end of month) Inventory at Cost ÷ 13 (months)

Gross Margin % = Gross Profit ÷ Gross Sales

Sales per visitor ($/V): This serves as a valuable measurement of your store's potential. The most accurate way to calculate this is to divide the number of visitors during open store hours for a period of time (day, week, month, year) by gross sales for the same time period. This is often used as a more realistic tool for forecasting your budget than a random percentage increase.

$/V = Gross Sales ÷ Number of Visitors

Capture rate: This is the percentage of museum visitors who make a purchase in the store. Tracking this can help you determine how interested museum visitors are in your store and how visible the store is. To calculate capture rate, use the following formula:

Capture Rate = Number of Transactions ÷ Number of Visitors

Where your store is located in the building or on the grounds can greatly affect capture rate. Although you may not be able to change locations, marketing, outreach, and better or more signage directing visitors to the store may help improve this figure.

Sales per square foot ($/f^2): Another important measurement of sales performance and profitability is sales per square foot. Because each square foot of retail space must be maintained, insured, and staffed, it's important that this space, in turn, yields a reasonable return. The standards for return vary from store to store, depending on, among other things, the nature of the merchandise and the varying overhead associated with different enterprises. Study industry averages to determine if your store is performing well. High sales per square foot can indicate healthy liquidity or well-used space. If $/f^2 is over industry averages, it is possible that this is not a healthy metric: your store may be losing sales because of overcrowding. Tracking $/f^2 has informed decisions to expand stores to be more profitable. Sales per square foot that are too high may indicate a need for more space. Low sales per square foot suggest an excess of retail space or an obsolete inventory. Are your sales performing well or struggling because it's too big, too small, or poorly laid out or has too much or too little merchandise? Ask sister institutions with similarities to give you $/f^2 benchmarks for your size and type of store. Bear in mind that book-heavy stores have a slightly lower figure than a store stocking more gift items.

If you note that your sales are not meeting the daily or monthly average needed to meet your budget projections, you can take steps immediately to change the course. The preceding metrics can guide you to make changes in displays, pricing, signage, and more. Your sales force is the driver, so include them in tracking progress toward the goal.

This is the easiest way to calculate sales per square foot:

$$\$/f^2 = \text{Net Sales} \div \text{Square Footage of Selling Space*}$$

*Selling space is the measurement of the areas where you sell plus the sales desk. It does not include offices, storage, warehouse, etc.

Inventory turnover: One of the most important ratio measures, inventory turnover, tells how many weeks or months it takes to sell the merchandise on hand. Because inventory represents a dollar investment, a good average turnover generally maximizes that investment. Too high a turn means you should order in more depth and take advantage of deeper discounts and less freight. Too low a turn means a slow-moving product that should probably be marked down and replaced with better merchandise. Inventory turnover is different for each category. For instance, books generally have a slower turn than jewelry. You can perform this analysis by category.

Although inventory turnover can be calculated for any period, it is generally calculated on an annual or quarterly basis.

Inventory Turnover = Net Sales ÷ Average Inventory at Retail

Average transaction: The average transaction is a good gauge of customers' overall reaction to your store. It also can indicate how well the store is merchandised to encourage add-on sales and the level of selling expertise of your staff. The POS report will give you the information you need on a daily, sometimes hourly, basis: total sales and total transactions. To determine sales per transaction:

Sales per Transaction = Net Sales ÷ Number of Transactions

Increasing your stores' sales per transaction figure is particularly useful when museum visitation is flat or falling. Even modest incremental increases to sales per transaction can add up over time to large increases in overall net sales.

Cost of goods sold as a percentage of net sales: By tracking cost of goods sold as a percentage of net sales, you can watch for subtle shifts that could end up eating into the store's profitability. An increase in net sales is generally seen as good, but if your cost of goods sold is rising at a higher rate, your store's performance could be in danger. Periodically track your cost of goods as a percentage of net sales using this formula:

Cost of Goods Sold (%) = Cost of Goods Sold ÷ Net Sales × 100

If this percentage is increasing, you may want to look at freight in costs to see if you can get lower shipping or reconsider your pricing strategy to compensate for higher costs.

Gross margin as a percentage of net sales: Gross margin indicates how profitable your operation is and, therefore, how much the store contributes back to the museum. By increasing your gross margin amount, you increase the amount of money that's left after paying for merchandise.

Increasing your gross margin as a percentage of net sales is even better because that means you're increasing your sales faster than you're increasing what you pay for merchandise.

Here's how you calculate it:

$$\text{Gross Margin as a Percentage of Net Sales} = \text{Gross Margin} \div \text{Net Sales} \times 100$$

You can usually increase your gross margin percentage by doing the following:

- Getting better prices on merchandise.
- Reducing shipping charges.
- Increasing the markup on merchandise.
- Selling more merchandise at full markup (rather than on sale).
- A combination of these factors.

METRICS VERSUS MISSION

Keep in mind that mission-driven museum initiatives can have an impact on KPIs for both revenue and expense lines of a retail budget. For example, stocking more inventory from local artisans and craftspeople may lower a store's gross margin even as it reduces freight costs and increases sales per square foot. Efforts to increase a store's accessibility and inclusivity may require taking on new expenses (American Sign Language training for staff, for example, or adding resources for staff and guests with vision impairment). There is no single right answer for a museum store's budget, but the budget stage is the opportunity to write into your business plan the initiatives outlined in your organization's strategic plan.

ESTABLISHING ACCOUNTING PROCEDURES AND MAINTAINING ACCURATE RECORDS

In many museums, the store's financial records are kept not by the store manager but by the institution's bookkeeping and accounting departments. However, your POS system keeps much of this information at your fingertips. That makes it convenient for a manager to track progress.

You want to track and continually compare the following:

- Daily, weekly, and monthly sales
- Current year-to-date sales versus prior sales
- Sales per visitor
- Average transaction
- Capture rate
- Cost of goods

You may want to build into your POS ways of tracking progress on mission-driven goals. For example, if you want to report the percentages of sustainable products sold in your store throughout the year, you need to add a field or qualifier to your POS to identify those items to be able to run the suitable report.

Work with your accounting department to set up your system. Templates may be found in your software. The line items of your budget should match all other spreadsheets in content and order. Depending on the size of your store's revenues and the complexity of its operations, your accounting department will establish either an accrual or cash basis system.

Note that, as tax-exempt enterprises, museum stores do not pay federal income tax on revenue designated "related" by Internal Revenue Service (IRS) standards. However, many local and state governments do levy a tax on all sales. Sales tax varies by city, county, and state. Check with your State Board of Equalization for the laws and rates in your area.

The federal government does levy income tax on what it calls unrelated business income (UBI) or income derived from sources that don't correspond with the organization's mission. If your store carries merchandise that doesn't relate to your mission, it is considered unrelated. This is not a sales tax. UBIT is calculated not on retail sales alone but in conjunction with all earned revenue of the nonprofit; activities such as building rentals can fall into this category too. Work with your accounting department to determine the desired balance of related and unrelated merchandise for your organization.

It is best to develop a method of identifying these products when receiving them in your inventory. On the inventory record, look for a reportable field that you can adapt to "Related: YES/NO." This way, at year end, it is easy to run a report of sales of all items marked "Related: NO" and forward it to your accounting department to be included with the rest of the organization's unrelated taxable income. (Note: It is not bad to have unrelated sales, just report them!)

PROFIT-AND-LOSS STATEMENTS

The profit-and-loss [P&L] statement, also called an income statement, records the store's monthly income and expenses and the resulting profit or loss. From this, a manager can study the store's performance and evaluate any necessary corrective action, such as reducing overhead or adjusting markup.

There are five key factors in the formulation of the P&L statement:

- Gross sales
- Cost of goods sold
- Gross profit
- Operating expenses
- Net profit

In addition to monthly P&L statements, you may, if appropriate, prepare a quarterly or annual year-end balance sheet and a statement of cash flow. Check with your accounting department to determine the necessity. Go to MSA's Resource Library on the website to download a sample profit and loss template.

BALANCE SHEET

The balance sheet presents the museum store's financial position at a specified date, such as at the end of the fiscal year. It lists the store's assets, liabilities, and fund balances.

Assets should include any resource or object of measurable financial value owned by the store. Assets can encompass everything from the petty cash fund to inventory and furniture. Some of these assets are depreciable, meaning that their cost is allocated over their useful life. Liabilities are financial claims on the assets by outsiders. These include any accounts payable or outstanding loan balances.

TRANSIENT RECORDS

Some records should be kept permanently, but others, known as transient records, should be purged periodically. When is it safe to throw out records? Check with your accounting department. They will determine the policy for record retention.

BUILDING ORGANIZATIONAL MISSION AND DEAI PRIORITIES INTO YOUR STORE'S BUDGET

Incorporate your organization's mission and DEAI priorities into your museum store's annual budget to ensure dedicated funding for these essential initiatives.

Begin by aligning your financial planning with your museum's overarching mission and DEAI goals. Evaluate how the store can advance these priorities and allocate budget resources. This may be through ensuring accessibility, updating technology, creating community events, or offering a diverse range of products. This may also include investing in staff training on DEAI principles. Regularly review the budget to reflect progress and emerging opportunities, ensuring that your store becomes an integral part of the museum's commitment to DEAI.

SUMMARY POINTS

- Budgets can provide a blueprint for sound fiscal policies.
- P&L statements can help you assess your store's financial state and take corrective action when necessary.
- Calculating and tracking key retail performance measurements help you compare your store's performance with past years and with other museum stores.

3

Point of Sale and e-Commerce

Chapter Highlights

- Choosing a POS system
- Credit cards
- PCI compliance
- Setting up an online store
- Developing an appealing, easy-to-navigate website
- Legal issues
- Accessibility online

A point-of-sale (POS) system is designed to streamline and manage retail transactions. In its most simple form, it is used to ring up sales at the point of purchase. It is the backbone of a museum store's sales processing, inventory management, and reporting.

It can also contain a customer relationship management (CRM) system that assists in customer service by taking names, mail and email addresses, and telephone numbers and uses this information for a variety of marketing initiatives. These systems maintain valuable data on customer preferences and purchase history, aiding in better informed business decisions and more efficient operations.

CHOOSING A POS SYSTEM

As you search for software and hardware, remember that the ideal POS system varies from user to user and from business to business. There is also a large number of POS options to choose from (such as Counterpoint, Retail Pro, Square, The Assistant Manager (TAM), Lightspeed, and Shopify).

The first step is to identify what you need by developing questions that address your expectations. It is a good idea to have input in creating a list of questions from the stakeholders who will be users of the systems, such as receiving and warehouse managers, accounting representatives, sales and staff supervisors, buyers, online sales managers, and the store manager or department head.

When choosing a system, create a list of features you require and rank them from necessary to desirable. Some features that are important to you may not be standard and cost extra. If the level of importance is high, be prepared to add it to the cost. Use the same capabilities to rate various systems. Look for pricing in relation to your annual revenue, scalability (ability to grow with your sales), hidden costs (upgrades, support, etc.), and compatibility with your organization's accounting software.

Visit the MSA Resource Library on the MSA website for more information, including POS checklists.

Sample questions

- Is it cloud-based, and is that vital to your organization? Do you have the Wi-Fi capabilities to support this?
- Is it maintained on a local server?
- Do you expect it to be a cash register with inventory reporting?
- Do you expect it to have handheld capabilities?
- Do you need multiple locations feeding data into a central server?
- Can it manage multiple discounts and identify them?
- What are the security levels?
- Does it offer technical support?
- Does it have a CRM system embedded?
- Does it have internal credit card processing?
- Is it compatible with your website?
- Is it compatible with your organization's accounting system?
- Do you need a remote location for entering purchase orders and receiving?
- What kind of information does each product include?
- What kind of daily/monthly/annual reports can it produce?
- Does it have inventory turnover calculation?
- Is there an open-to-buy (OTB) calculator?
- Does it have reportable fields to handle relatedness status?
- Can inventory be connected to your online store?

REPORTS

There are a variety of reports available you may need from your POS system. Thoroughly research what you and your accounting department may need. The following are some basic reports:

- Daily sales
- Discounts
- Sales tax
- Totals by type of tender (cash, checks, credit/debit cards)
- Sales associate ID number by transaction
- Number of transactions by tender
- Sales by time of day
- Sales by category (books, gifts, paper goods, jewelry, etc.)
- Sales by vendor
- Petty cash
- Inventory by category on hand
- Purchase orders (receivables)
- Receiving log (invoices reconciled to purchase orders and date sent to accounts payable)

Make sure your system is supported by a vendor who answers your questions, resolves your problems quickly, and meets the special needs of your store. Your vendor should be flexible and accommodating as long as it does not compromise the system's integrity or accuracy.

Many cloud-based solutions are updated automatically and rely on a series of "how-to" videos for support and training. Other POS systems may no longer staff technicians to answer questions or may charge per contact. Consider if your operation is set up to handle this or is in need of more specialized support and training.

Each POS system is unique in its user experience and offerings. Refer to your POS manual or contact your representative for assistance.

CREDIT CARDS

Credit card sales are a vital part of the museum store business. It is required that all credit card information be secured. Your processor handles this. Maintain communication with your processing provider to stay current on credit card and security requirements.

You need to set up a merchant account and lease or buy credit card terminals. Some companies charge application and setup costs. Be sure that your credit card processing provider is compatible with your POS system.

Typically, a store is responsible for monthly fees as well as transaction fees and discount rates on each transaction. The fees are usually based on the store's sales volume, although if other areas of the museum accept credit cards (admissions, food service), you may be able to negotiate a better rate if you use the same bank for all transactions.

The transaction fee is usually a set amount per completed transaction, whereas the discount rate is a percentage of the sale that the merchant service provider keeps as a handling fee. Most companies charge different discount rates for transactions in which cards are processed through a terminal versus when the card is not present. The latter transactions carry a higher risk of fraud, and therefore credit card companies charge higher fees for them.

Fees and rates can vary widely, so check with several merchant service providers to get the best deal based on the characteristics and needs of your store and institution. Lowering your per-transaction fee or discount rate by just a small amount can have a large impact if your customers often use credit cards.

PAYMENT CARD INDUSTRY (PCI) COMPLIANCE

The Payment Card Industry Data Security Standard (PCI DSS) is a set of security standards and practices designed to protect sensitive financial data, such as credit card information, during and after payment transactions. PCI compliance is crucial for any organization that processes or stores credit card data to prevent data breaches and maintain the trust of customers.

Although it is not a law, the steps a business must take to be PCI compliant are in the terms of the contract or agreement with its merchant or payment service provider and the card networks. Work with your IT departments to become compliant. Being PCI noncompliant can lead to your organization facing fines from payment processors and credit card processing restrictions.

Visit the PCI Security Standards Council website (www.pcisecuritystandards .org) for more information.

SETTING UP AN ONLINE STORE

Most museum stores rely heavily on visitation to achieve their revenue targets. However, in response to this challenge, many have adopted a strategy of diversifying their income sources by establishing online stores.

This transition to e-commerce offers a multitude of advantages:

- It can be inexpensive to set up and maintain.
- It offers the ability to reach a global market and expand awareness of its products and brand identities.
- Because an online store is visual and text driven, it offers an opportunity to tell a richer story about the products than may be possible in the store.
- It is a form of advertising the on-site store. Some people look at the online store as they plan their visit and then come in and make purchases.
- It adds revenue that is not dependent on museum visitors.

Development and maintenance costs vary widely, but e-commerce continues to become more cost effective. The cost can be even more attractive when viewed as an alternative to printing an extensive, full-color catalog.

Online stores do not have to represent every item in your inventory. In fact, they can be launched with only twenty-five to fifty items that showcase your product selection. You can add and remove items as sales develop and you gain a clearer idea of what your online customer is looking for.

When initially choosing your online store, you have several options to consider. Before moving forward, consider your budget along with your store's and institution's needs.

The following are some factors to keep in mind when planning budgets:

- E-commerce platforms: Choose an e-commerce platform or software that suits your museum's needs. Some options include Shopify, WooCommerce, BigCommerce, and Magento (now Adobe Commerce). These platforms provide templates, inventory management, and payment processing.
- Custom website development: For a more tailored website, you can hire a web developer to build a custom e-commerce site tailored to your museum's specific requirements. This option allows for more flexibility and customization but requires continual investment in custom web development to maintain and keep your website up to date with changing devices, web software platforms, and e-commerce standards.
- Payment processing: Choose a payment gateway that is secure and aligns with your business needs. Factor credit card fees into your budget.
- Inventory management: Will your e-commerce inventory sync to your POS inventory? Make a plan for how to manage your e-commerce inventory.
- Shipping and fulfillment: Decide how you will handle shipping and fulfillment. You can manage it in house, work with a fulfillment center, or use drop shipping if applicable. Before you put up an online store, research and make a policy for international shipping.
- User experience and mobile optimization: Ensure your online store is user friendly and mobile responsive. Most shoppers access e-commerce websites from mobile devices.
- Security and privacy: Prioritize security measures to protect customer data and transactions. Secure sockets layer (SSL) certificates, secure payment gateways, and compliance with data protection regulations are essential.
- Membership: If you have a membership, there is built-in loyalty. Will your website be able to offer member discounts online?
- Gift cards: If your store sells gift cards, will your website be able to accept them as payment?

DEVELOPING AN APPEALING, EASY-TO-NAVIGATE WEBSITE

RESEARCH OTHER SITES

To gain clarity about the look, feel, and navigation of your site, visit other e-commerce pages for other museum stores and speak to your colleagues about the pros and cons of what they have chosen. Don't forget to include for-profit retail sites to see what works well and what doesn't.

USER EXPERIENCE

Concentrate on creating a site that provides a great user experience (UX) by providing easy navigation and checkout capabilities. This includes having a website that is mobile compatible and loads quickly.

It is recommended that you use a commercial template rather than have a custom shop built. If your online store is custom, you are reliant on the builder for upgrades, changes, and fixing glitches. Using a template doesn't mean you lose individuality. Many platforms (such as Shopify, Squarespace, Woo-Commerce, and Wix) allow you to create a look that reflects your institution's website brand and style.

DESIGN FACTORS

Don't overdo graphics and animations. Your page should look attractive, professional, and interesting, but complex graphics can take too long to load. One study estimates that you have only eight seconds in which to capture interest before the visitor leaves, so make a great opening impression.

Whereas elaborate displays of products can intrigue a visitor to visit an on-site store, online shoppers may be less interested in complex presentations and more interested in understanding the product that they are looking at. In many ways, this style of shopping forces the design, fabrication, and pricing of a product to stand on its own.

Keep in mind integration with your institution's website. Ensure a seamless integration between your museum's main website and the online store, maintaining a consistent brand and user experience.

PRODUCT SELECTION

Make an assessment of the products you will offer online or are likely to offer in the future. They should be visually compelling, proven sellers, and easy to understand. Your text description has to act as the sales associate in your store explaining the virtues of a product. Write concise and compelling copy that gives details such as color choices and dimensions. If possible, add a short video to the product page that demonstrates the item.

When posting, ensure that you have clear, high-resolution photography of your products. Often vendors will supply photography of their products. Invest in photography to make your products appealing to online shoppers and create a visually stunning experience.

CUSTOMER SERVICE

Customer service extends to your online store. Provide email, chat, or phone number options for customers to receive help with orders, questions, and the inevitable lost package.

Be sure to disclose refund and return policies on your site and address customer privacy. Tell your site visitors what information you are collecting and how you use it.

SITE OPERATION AND MAINTENANCE

Keep your site fresh and up to date. As with a physical store, you can leave up certain product staples, but changes keep people coming back to see what's new.

LEGAL ISSUES

Specify where you're doing business. Unless you post notices to the contrary, you're selling "everywhere." The European Union and many individual countries have specific laws and requirements for how e-commerce is conducted. Contact government sources that set rules where you do business to find out if other local, regional, or national restrictions might apply. Work with your accounting department and stay informed about applicable tax laws.

ACCESSIBILITY ONLINE

Museums have a unique opportunity to bridge the gap between cultural heritage and all individuals regardless of their abilities. To make these digital spaces truly inclusive, prioritize accessibility for people with disabilities. Ensuring that the website is accessible is a legal requirement. Keep up to date with web accessibility standards and guidelines, such as the Web Content Accessibility Guidelines (WCAG), and ensure your website complies with the latest recommendations.

One fundamental step in ensuring accessibility is the incorporation of alternative text (alt text) and accessible image captions. Alt text provides a textual description of images on the website, ensuring that individuals with visual impairments can understand the visual content. It's essential that these descriptions are not only comprehensive but also clear and concise, allowing for a smooth and meaningful experience.

Another important factor is implementing a responsive website that adapts to various screen sizes and devices, ensuring that users with disabilities, including those who use screen readers or magnification software, can access your website on both desktop and mobile platforms. Screen readers are software programs that allow blind or visually impaired users to read the text that is displayed on the computer screen with a speech synthesizer or braille display.

Moreover, conducting regular accessibility audits of the museum's online store on both desktop and mobile views is essential. This audit ensures that the website's structure, layout, and content are compatible with screen readers, guaranteeing that pages can be accurately translated for individuals who rely on these services. Use accessibility evaluation tools and user testing and seek feedback from your audience to identify and address accessibility issues. By making these accommodations, online museum stores promote an inclusive and equal experience for all visitors, fostering a sense of belonging and accessibility to cultural and artistic offerings.

In addition to legal and ethical considerations, accessibility features not only improve the overall user experience but also expand the potential visitor base for online museum stores. Many individuals with disabilities are eager to engage with cultural and artistic content, and by removing digital barriers, museums can tap into a previously underserved audience. Beyond that, embracing accessibility showcases a commitment to diversity, inclusion, and equitable access, which can bolster a museum's reputation and foster goodwill among the public. In an era when the digital landscape is integral to the dissemination of culture and knowledge, museums that ensure accessibility are poised to make a more significant and lasting impact on society.

SUMMARY POINTS

- Choose a POS system that fits your store's needs.
- An online presence expands awareness of your products and brand identities.
- Keep your budget in mind when planning and developing your online store.

4

Merchandise Planning and Management

Chapter Highlights

- Developing a sound merchandise plan
- Considering DEAI in your merchandise plan
- Merchandise selection, pricing, and margin
- Exploring product resources
- Product development and licensing
- Using open-to-buy
- Inventory turnover
- Managing your inventory and inventory counts

Merchandise represents a retailer's most significant investment. The selection, management, and control of that merchandise constitute the heart of any retail operation. An initial assumption is that the selection in the store is related closely to the mission and exhibits in the museum and meets unrelated business income tax guidelines (covered in chapter 2).

DEVELOPING A SOUND MERCHANDISE PLAN

Crucial decisions regarding the store's ambiance and character must be carefully considered. What will be the quality, price range, and focus of the product selection? Which product categories will command what percentage of the floor space and inventory dollars? How will the values of the museum be expressed in the retail selection? To decide this, it is important to know who your visitor is. Your marketing department has likely spent a great deal of time analyzing this because it is critical to the way it spends advertising dollars. Consult with your marketing team and examine its data to make informed choices and target the best price point of products.

MERCHANDISE PLAN

The first step in preparing a merchandise plan is a projection of sales and of the supporting stock that can be reasonably expected during a specified period. When carefully crafted, the merchandise plan makes a useful tool for meeting a sales plan and adjusting to promotional efforts. Without a carefully formulated merchandise plan, you won't be prepared for brisk sales seasons or special events. The merchandise plan also provides a means of keeping the inventory investment under control so that stock turnover allows for a profit.

The basic elements of a merchandise plan are net sales, stock on hand, markdowns, and purchases. When preparing your merchandise plan, be sure to do the following:

- Map it out six months in advance of its effective date.
- Keep it simple.
- Forecast over the entire fiscal year, periodically reviewing the plan and making necessary adjustments.
- Allow for flexibility.
- Consider internal trends, including the long-term growth rate of sales and any conditions within the business that could influence future sales.
- Take into account external conditions, such as the economy, changing demographics in the region, added competition from new retailers, and changing fashions.

CONSIDERING DEAI IN YOUR MERCHANDISE PLANNING

The product selection in your store tells your audience about your museum's mission and ethics. To support your buying choices, take time to define goals, priorities, and considerations in advance of filling your product categories. Questions to pose when drawing up your merchandise plan include but are not limited to the following:

- How are diverse cultures within your community represented in the products offered in your retail store? To what extent are minority voices and perspectives included in your buying decisions?
- Is it important for a percentage of sales to come from a specific origin, such as local manufacturers or Black-owned businesses?
- What sensitivities does your buying team need to consider around reproducing or referencing objects in your museum's collections, such as artifacts from colonized communities, religious artwork presented in a secular context, culturally appropriated objects, or human remains?

- In what way are people with physical disabilities and sensitivities considered in your merchandise selection?

After investigating these questions, establish guidelines for buying and product development that are consistent with your museum's mission, clear, and easy to follow.

MERCHANDISE SELECTION, PRICING, AND MARGIN

MERCHANDISE SELECTION

Choosing merchandise is one of the most exciting aspects of managing a museum store. It can also be a complex and tricky process. Although vendors and products are seemingly endless, selecting just the right merchandise requires retail savvy, planning, and careful consideration. Keep in mind that good buyers do not buy to their own tastes but to the mission of their organization and to their customer profile.

If you cater mostly to children, buy quality items that they can afford and that will appeal to their parents and grandparents. Consider also your store's traditional merchandise mix. If you carry a variety of products—everything from jewelry to books—know which items are the most popular and which appeal to a select clientele. Buy accordingly.

If you're testing a new product or product line, decide carefully and order a sufficient quantity to make a statement, remembering to do the following:

- Look for merchandise that relates to your museum's collections and exhibits and enhances its educational mission.
- Choose only well-designed, carefully crafted products as shoddy merchandise reflects not only on your store but also on the museum.
- Consider how you will display a particular item and if you might need to invest in suitable display fixtures.
- Resist the temptation to buy too broadly, sticking to a few key products that complement the rest of your inventory.
- Order small numbers of high-priced items that tend to turn over slowly, and consider ordering inexpensive children's items in quantity.

To make certain your selection in any product category meets your customers' needs, it is helpful to create a product selection matrix to guide your purchases. The upper horizontal axis of the matrix lists all the characteristics for a product category or subcategory that should be fulfilled by the products available in that category. Using books as an example, these characteristics might include the following:

- Hardback and softcover
- Price ranges

- Reading ability levels
- Subject categories

The vertical axis would include the titles of all books or groups of similar books. For each item on the vertical axis, place an "X" under each characteristic the book fulfills. When the matrix is completed, it is easy to spot characteristics that are not fulfilled by a sufficient number of books or those for which there are too many titles. Then you can make adjustments as additional stock is purchased.

For new or expanding stores, complete the matrix during the product selection process and before purchase orders are prepared. All products should be reviewed and sales analyzed on a monthly basis before reordering or expanding a category.

BUYING BOOKS

The first step in purchasing books is to become familiar with the various publishing houses and distributors (including other museums) and their titles. Get on their mailing lists and peruse their catalogs carefully. You might also want to join the American Booksellers Association. Other resources are Edelweiss Books and Books in Print (www.booksinprint.com), an online service that tells you which titles are available, who publishes or distributes them, how much they cost, and whether they are printed in paperback or hardback. Books are indexed according to title, author, and subject. When ordering books, consider all the resources at your disposal. In addition to publishing houses, which may offer cooperative advertising incentives, quality books are available from the following:

- Distributors purchase books from a variety of publishers and provide one shipment and, thus, one invoice for a variety of titles.
- Publishers' reps handle a group of publishers and can often show you smaller, more obscure presses that carry gems in the museum world and won't be found in standard bookstores.
- University and museum presses offer quality volumes on a variety of topics.

Whereas general merchandise items, such as gifts and jewelry, are priced at wholesale, allowing retailers to set the selling price, book prices are generally set by the publisher, and wholesale costs are based on a discount off the retail. The discount increases as the number of books (combined titles) you purchase increases. Request each publisher's trade discount schedule from which you can determine the price you will pay for each book.

Many publishers take back books in good condition for full credit. To take advantage of return policies, you need to get a return authorization and supply the original invoice number. Many publishers also offer nonreturnable discounts, which are higher than standard discounts. If you are convinced a title will sell well, enhance your profits by purchasing it at the nonreturnable discount price.

Whereas books represent a very important line in museum stores, it can be challenging to make money if books comprise a very high percentage of your sales. Freight charges on books are often high, and the markup on books is usually lower than the markup on any other merchandise category in your store.

Be on the lookout for bargains. Most publishers offer sales once or twice a year when discounts are higher and sometimes freight is free.

Remainder houses offer books that did not sell well from publishers and wholesalers at a sizable discount, but books may not be returned.

RETAIL PRICING

Determining the retail price structure for the store should precede the buying and retail pricing of merchandise. Run reports from your inventory control system to determine at which price point the store is selling the most merchandise. This will vary depending on the type of institution and the profile of the visitor. Look for a fresh product mix that retails within a range of that price point.

Part of the retail pricing process is to find products that, when the retail price is determined through whatever method, fulfill the objectives of the pricing plan. This process requires you to determine at least a close approximation of the retail price before you order a product.

There is no single formula for pricing. Although cost is the major factor, the price should reflect a number of valuation variables. Keep the following in mind:

- To a consumer, price measures the value of an item.
- Price is a psychological measure of the quality of an item.
- Price reflects the relationship of an item to comparable products, so if it's more expensive, it may appear superior, and if it's less expensive, it may appear inferior.
- Product uniqueness can push prices up, and a wide variety of substitute products limits the maximum price.
- Large items require lots of space, commanding a larger chunk of overhead, so the price should incorporate the fixed cost associated with storage and display.
- The income of clientele and the health of the economy determine price, resulting in increased spending on luxury items when income increases.
- Prices usually rise with demand.

  To determine markup, retailers use various pricing strategies

- Keystoning: Doubling the wholesale cost. This is no longer a commonly used strategy as it does not always have a sufficient markup

- Penetration: Starting out with a low price to capture market share quickly. Profitability depends on a high volume of sales. The price can rise as demand increases. This works best in markets with high repeat purchase rates.
- Loss leaders: Selling a high-volume item at or below cost to attract customers. Works only when likely to drive up demand for the remaining inventory.
- Bundling: Assign one price to items when sold singly. Assign a lower price when sold with other items. This allows you to move more merchandise than you might ordinarily while still charging a respectable price.
- Manufacturer's suggested retail price (MSRP): The price that a manufacturer recommends a retail business charge for a product.
- Cost-plus pricing: When a seller determines the retail price of a product by adding a markup cost, usually by a percentage of the cost or a flat fee.
- Value-based pricing: Determining the retail price of a product based on the perceived value to the customer.

Regardless of the method, some modern retail pricing theory suggests the cost basis on which to base markup should include the following:

- The cost of the item
- Freight in
- Import duties
- Customs fees
- Special packaging needs
- The cost of taking the product from the back door through the receiving process and getting it on the shelf

Retailers often use prices ending in .99 or .95 because it creates a psychological effect, making the product appear slightly cheaper to consumers. Conversely, prices ending in .00 are often used to convey a sense of quality and luxury, suggesting that the product is premium and worth the higher cost.

Whichever pricing rules you decide to use within your store, the key is to stay consistent.

MARGINS

In rough terms, margin is the difference between the costs associated with buying and bringing in a product and the selling price. Margins vary as some products command significantly higher margins than others. Typically, books offer lower margins. Impulse, novelty items, souvenirs, unique and handcrafted products, and jewelry generally have higher margins.

Think about margins before you buy. This way, you can strike a blended margin among all product categories that maximizes the margin for the store as a whole. The formula to determine margins is

$$Margin = Selling\ Price - Cost + Freight\ In$$

EXPLORING PRODUCT RESOURCES

TRADE SHOWS

Many museum store managers buy their merchandise at trade shows, such as the MSA Expo, which afford the luxury of one-stop shopping and provide a valuable opportunity for studying new products. You can either place orders at the show or pick up catalogs and order forms for later purchases. Attending trade shows allows you to do the following:

- Identify merchandising trends.
- Compare merchandise and examine it for quality and workmanship.
- Meet manufacturers and occasionally even product designers.
- Gain helpful sales, merchandising, and display tips for establishing a long-term relationship with suppliers.
- Take advantage of or negotiate pricing discounts and/or shipping charges.

Before attending a trade show or placing a catalog order, it's important to know the following:

- How much money you need to spend
- How much merchandise you need
- What kind of merchandise you need to buy
- When you need the merchandise

For more information on merchandise planning, see the OTB section of this chapter.

You need to prepare a credit sheet for any new vendors from which you may order. This will help you avoid many of the problems that often arise with the opening of new accounts. Often vendors prefer to be paid with a purchasing card (company credit card).

A credit sheet should include the following:

- Store name and billing address
- Museum name, address, and phone number
- Shipping address

- Names of the buyer or store manager
- Name, address, and telephone number of your bank
- Your account number
- The date that your store opened for business (the standard phrasing is "operating since . . .")
- the store's tax-exempt numbers (your accountant can provide these)
- Credit references: preferably three vendors with whom you have done business

Vendors may prefer to have purchases made using a credit card (company credit for the express purpose of making approved purchases).

If you choose to order from a new vendor, be sure to ask some key questions:

- Do they offer special show discounts?
- How will they ship the merchandise? (Always make sure vendors use the most economical shipping means, and if you have special preferences, specify these on the purchase order.)
- Prepare and deliver a copy of your terms and conditions for purchasing. A purchase order is a binding contract when signed.
- Many vendors are using electronic tablets to write orders. Be prepared with an email address to have your order transmitted.
- When will they ship the merchandise? (To avoid costly misunderstandings, include a cancellation date on the order.)
- When will you be billed?
- When will payment be due?
- Does the product come with information for descriptive cards, which helps to connect the product to the mission of the museum?

Show tips: Although trade shows provide wonderful opportunities for stocking your store with quality merchandise, they can be overwhelming. Equip yourself to get the most from a trade show experience. Seasoned buyers recommend the following for new buyers:

- Go to the trade show's website before going to the show and note vendors that interest you, show specials, etc.
- Review the show catalog before walking the floor to become familiar with the exhibits and prepare yourself for sensory overload.
- Walk the entire floor before placing any orders.
- On your initial survey of the floor, spend no more than five minutes at any booth.
- Pay special attention to booths with crowds as these often offer trendsetting merchandise.

- Take a good-size tote or rolling bag for the brochures and catalogs you'll acquire.
- Take a calculator and calendar to help you track how much you've spent and to schedule deliveries.
- In addition to a credit sheet, it is a good idea to prepare a sheet to give to new vendors that outline all the necessary functions for you to accept the shipment. This should include carriers, packing lists, substitutions, and ship/cancellation dates.
- Dress professionally, but wear comfortable shoes.
- Stick to your merchandise plan.
- Be open to finding new and exciting products that will set your store above the rest and strongly support the look and mission of your organization.

Before asking the cost of a product or making the decision to buy it, try to determine what it can retail for in your store (excluding those products that are prepriced). After you determine what your market will bear, ask about the wholesale price. If the wholesale price is not low enough for you to maintain your margin objectives, move on to another product or vendor. The time to determine the retail price of a product is before it is purchased, not when it arrives at your store.

A word of caution about buying at shows: it is easy to get caught up in the excitement of a show; show discounts, free freight, volume discounts, and other specials available during the show are enticing. Many of these specials are valuable and should be used to your advantage. A leading cause of overbuying, however, is the excessive use of these specials, which results in overstocking. The discounting of this overstock often results in losses of revenue that exceed the initial savings from the special offers and, in the meantime, ties up valuable inventory dollars. Be strategic; many vendors will give you a special discount for writing the order at the show but will agree to later and/or staggered delivery dates.

ONLINE WHOLESALE MARKETPLACES

Online wholesale marketplaces (such as Faire, Brandwise, Handshake, Abound, and many more) have taken wholesale merchandise sourcing online. These platforms provide a vast array of products and brands, making finding new and relevant items accessible to museum store managers right from your computer. To effectively utilize these platforms, start by creating an account and familiarizing yourself with the marketplace's features, terms, payment methods, and return policies. If possible, order samples from vendors. Though purchasing online brings ease to the process, it can be difficult to know the size and quality of an item without interacting with it before purchasing.

CONSIGNMENT MERCHANDISE

To broaden a merchandise mix without dipping into cash sources and to reduce the risk associated with new artists and artistic product lines, museum stores may sell products on consignment. Consignment means that, rather than buying the goods outright, the store displays merchandise and retains a percentage of the selling price, and the remainder goes to the producer. If the items do not sell, they remain the property of the producer.

Artists and craftspeople often sell on consignment. This offers the store manager or buyer opportunities to carry products with special local or topical significance at less cost and risk. These items reside in your inventory as long as you have them at the amount it will cost when you sell. If you do not sell them and return the product, it should be taken out of your inventory. Everything comes at a cost, however. The tradeoff for not purchasing the inventory is generally a lower profit. The maker usually keeps a majority percentage of the sale and often dictates the selling price.

Consignment arrangements should be considered carefully. Give some thought to the following:

- Are the items related to the museum's collection and focus?
- Will the store receive enough revenue to justify the space for displaying the piece?
- Will insurance cover any loss or damage to the property?

The benefits of selling consignment merchandise include offering one-of-a-kind pieces that often appeal to customers and no money invested in the inventory.

The disadvantages may include special display and security arrangements, detailed bookkeeping procedures to log consignment sales and calculate payment to the artist, special care and maintenance for artworks of varying composition that might have to be returned to the artist, and generally lower profit margin.

Just as a purchase order is a contract between your store and a trade vendor, a written and signed consignment agreement between the store and the artist is required. This contains liability and avoids potential misunderstandings and conflicts. The law typically requires retailers to pay the artist within a certain time after the sale. The store is responsible for insuring the work. Often makers are not business savvy and may not be prepared with an agreement or even an invoice. Selling their work is a wonderful way of supporting the arts, and being prepared to handle paperwork helps them learn about doing business and assures them of fair treatment.

Consignment arrangements should be made in the form of a contract, a confirmation letter, or an order form that states the product description, quantity, price, shipping terms, and who controls the product's display and merchandising. Be sure to include information on deadlines for pickup and forfeiture by the artist. Find sample consignment agreements on the MSA website's MSA Resource Library.

OTHER MERCHANDISE SOURCES

For other ideas on merchandise, consult with store managers from museums with similar collections, programs, and missions. They often buy from vendors who do not exhibit at trade shows. Consider the following:

- Read trade magazines, which carry advertisements and articles that feature new and innovative products.
- Scout the competition by visiting commercial and other museum stores inside and out of your trade area with similar product lines.
- Attend the MSA Expo and talk to vendors geared for museum stores.
- See what wholesale products are being made at your peer institutions that are appropriate for your store.
- Build a good relationship with reputable product reps who are interested in your long-term success, not just in selling their product lines.
- Review commercial mail-order catalogs to see which products are repeated from catalog to catalog, which is a good indicator that the items produce steady sales.
- Check e-commerce sites to see what is being offered at the retail sites.

PRODUCT DEVELOPMENT AND LICENSING

PRODUCT DEVELOPMENT

Visitors to museums often want souvenirs or reproductions of items on display. Producing your own products is a complex undertaking, one that requires a large investment of money, storage space for increased inventory, considerable research, and careful thought.

The most common product developed by those beginning a product development program is a line of postcards and note cards featuring prominent selections from the collection.

Before contracting for reproductions of any kind, find out if your museum owns the copyright to a particular piece. Owning the piece does not mean owning the right to reproduce it. If not, you have to negotiate permission from the rightsholder and may have to pay a fee or royalty. This must be documented in a letter of agreement or contract. Check with your legal department or consultant. The registrar's office generally holds all the rights information.

Many managers of small shops shy away from custom product offerings, fearing that the cost will be prohibitive. However, these types of investments can be surprisingly cost effective. T-shirts, mugs, tote bags, and even imprinted pencils with the museum's logo or perhaps a reference to the more popular exhibits are easily and inexpensively procured in most local markets. Vendors generally charge an initial setup fee and retain the setup for future production runs. Large-quantity ordering for an entire season keeps costs down, and minor changes such as a date or feature can keep subsequent production runs fresh with minimal incremental expense. Digital technology has greatly reduced the need for large-quantity printed products, which makes it more manageable for a small store.

If you plan to develop a line of products, the following guidelines will help:

- Talk to the curator and director about objects that can be used, remembering that the most important items in a collection might not be the most popular with the buying public. Valuable sources for finding objects that are popular with the public are docents, tour guides, and security officers. They are feet-on-the-ground observers of your visitors.
- Decide on design themes or images that best represent your collection and that have the most appeal to your customers.
- Determine the kind of product you will make.
- Prepare a budget:
  - Calculate the quantities required and compare those estimates with the quantities that need to be produced to secure a reasonable cost per item.
  - Obtain estimates for printing and packaging costs.
- Select a photographer with extensive experience in high-resolution digital photography for publications and reproductions. (Consult other local museums for referrals.)
- Select a printer whose estimates and quality best suit your needs.
- Contract a graphic artist to prepare a digital file of the image and text layout to send to the printer.
  - Be sure that the art is color-approved by your curator.
  - If it has been published in a brochure or book, use the same digital file because it has been preapproved.
  - Ask the registrar or curatorial department if restrictions have been put on the image, such as no full bleeds, cropping, or printing text on top of an image.
  - Curatorial may want to approve the "tombstone," identifying text you print.
  - Determine all costs for the graphic designer services before contracting. Ask how many revisions are covered in the fee.
- Set a schedule for the various stages of the project.

- Once the design has been given to the printer, stay on top of the product by checking a printed copy for color and printing quality and authorizing a final printing only when you are satisfied that the quality matches the production print.
- Evaluate packaging options. (Printers can shrink-wrap a product at low cost, but for an alternative packing design, collect estimates from packaging firms.)
- Set a retail price that includes all costs. If the selling price is high, revise the budget to make it more cost effective; if the selling price is unreasonable, end the project.
- Determine the life of the product: how long you will keep it in inventory and the rate you will mark down if they are not good sellers or temporary products.
- Plan for regular reprint runs to keep the products in stock if successful.

PUBLISHING

If publishing books falls under your purview, be knowledgeable about the publishing industry. This is different from the production of hard goods. Copublishing arrangements often are made with scholarly and specialized presses. For example, a science museum might contract with a publisher specializing in natural history. In a typical copublishing agreement, the museum provides the manuscript and digital files for the images and has design approval. The publisher typically edits and produces the manuscript and distributes the book.

Such a collaboration allows you to do the following:

- Share the risks and costs with another party.
- Tap into the publisher's distribution and marketing systems.
- Rely on the publisher to store and reorder the product.

LICENSING YOUR PRODUCTS

Licensing involves the development, with a manufacturer or publisher, of a product to be offered to retailers as part of a merchandise line. It is different from custom product development as it is available not just to your store but to retailers outside your own institution.

The item or line of items will generally carry the name of your institution (the licensed trademark) and images or a design generated or provided by your museum. The institution, as the actual or a third-party right holder, gives the manufacturer the right to use its name, mark, or images on a product. In return for the license, your museum receives a percentage based on the product sales. Royalties generated are a nice dividend, but the longer lasting, more important benefit is the increased recognition and branding of your institution and mission.

Licensing can be successful if

- your institution has a recognized and valued name,
- the images/artists/makers/inventors/authors are widely recognized and appreciated,
- you retain rights management for the images used, or
- you choose a licensee with a proven record of strong sales.

Remember: Clear the rights of the images! Owning the objects does not necessarily give your institution the copyright. It is important to know intellectual property and work with departments that can verify copyrights.

LICENSING PARTNERS

Licensee candidates are often companies with which you work already. These relationships provide a good foundation on which to build. Many companies are actively seeking partners in cause-related marketing from the nonprofit world. If you have an idea that will work for them, they will listen.

The match between each company and your institution must be right. Your licensing partner should have a quality product, a good business reputation, and business philosophies or actions that are compatible with your organization's mission.

The licensee should be in a prominent position to market and sell your licensed product and to give it good exposure. Ask for a marketing plan for your licensed products. The manufacturer is highly motivated to market and sell the products with your licensed images. Consider them a strong partner in promoting your brand and earning revenue for your organization.

In analyzing a potential licensing arrangement, ask yourself these important questions:

- How big is the licensee's distribution network?
- Does the company exhibit its products at trade shows? Which ones?
- Does it have road reps?
- Does it have a good catalog and website?
- How widespread are the company's wholesale clients?
- What kinds of stores carry its merchandise?
- Will other products they sell complement your product line?

LICENSING AGREEMENTS

You need to work out the specific details of any agreement. Among other things, there must be

- a written contract specifying the obligations and rights of both parties,
- a statement as to what exactly is being licensed,

- the percentage of royalty rate or other form of payment with definition of the rate (example: royalty = % of net sales),
- any advances,
- territory covered,
- right to inspect the licensee's financial records,
- right to periodically and randomly inspect products for quality,
- statement from licensee about legal and healthy working conditions in their manufactory,
- term of the agreement,
- right to renew or cancel the contract on termination date, and
- a nonexclusive contract.

It is vital to determine who will negotiate and monitor the agreement and who will ultimately sign the contract and administer the program.

For guidance on licensing contracts, contact a trademark or intellectual property attorney or qualified and experienced paralegal and check with other museum licensors.

USING OPEN-TO-BUY

One of the best merchandise planning systems is known as open-to-buy (OTB) or planned purchasing. OTB refers to the amount of merchandise that the buyer is open to receiving into inventory during a prescribed period and is based on planned sales, usually broken out into merchandise categories. The OTB figure shows how much merchandise can be received in the course of a month without exceeding the store's planned stock level.

The advantages of the OTB system are many. Foremost, it allows management to meet sales demands with a minimum of shortages and without

PLANNING WORKSHEET FOR OPEN-TO-BUY (OTB)

FISCAL YEAR:														
	DEC	JAN	FEB	MAR	APR	MAY	JUN	JUL	AUG	SEP	OCT	NOV	DEC	TOTAL
BOM														
SALES(-)														
MARKDOWNS(-)														
SUBTOTAL (=)														
PLANNED PURCHASES (+)														
EOM (=)														
PLANNED INVENTORY (-)														
+/- OTB (=)														
STOCK-TO-SALES RATIO:						AVERAGE INVENTORY:								
MARKDOWN %:						TURNOVER:								

Figure 4.1.   Planning Worksheet for Open-to-Buy (OTB). *The Museum Store Association*

excessive inventory levels. This enables the store to maximize efficiency and profits.

Today, many POS systems have built-in OTB management that calculates your OTB using data in its system. If your POS software does not have this capability, determining the OTB figure is relatively easy. First determine the planned purchases: add together planned sales, planned stock reductions, and planned end-of-month stock to learn your total needs for the month. Then subtract the planned beginning-of-month stock to determine planned purchases. The merchandise on order then must be subtracted from planned purchases. The resulting number is your OTB.

Find sample OTB worksheets on the MSA website's MSA Resource Library.

INVENTORY TURNOVER

Inventory turnover is a measurement of the efficient use of inventory dollars. Tracking and taking inventory will help you gauge inventory turnover and give you the data to know how many weeks or months it takes to sell the merchandise on hand.

Establishing definitive benchmarks for high or low turnover can be challenging. The rate of turnover is influenced by any number of variables. For example, high-end, handcrafted goods or books might not turn over nearly as fast as a line of note cards. As a result, your store's standards for high and low turnover benchmarks must be established for each product line. The formula for determining turnover is

Inventory Turnover = Annual Cost of Goods
Sold ÷ Average Inventory at Cost

[Average Inventory = (Beginning Inventory + Ending Inventory) ÷ 2]

For example, if the average inventory is $100,000 and the annual cost of goods sold is $270,000, the inventory turnover is 2.7 times per year:

2.7 = $270,000 ÷ 100,000

Once you've established standards, you will be able to better analyze inventory turnover.

High inventory turnover can be a sign of

- healthy liquidity,
- excellent product selection and merchandising,
- proactive customer service and selling, and
- understocking, which means you are sacrificing potential sales.

Low inventory turnover can be a sign of

- poor liquidity;
- overstocking, which means a waste of investment dollars;
- obsolescence; and
- a planned inventory build-up.

Although inventory turnover can be calculated for any period in general, it is calculated monthly. Turnover can be determined for your total stock on hand, for a line of merchandise, or even for a single item. Knowing turnover can help you determine what your correct stock level should be, exactly where you are overstocked or understocked, and what you should do about it. Not all products have the same inventory turnover. Note what appears to be a healthy turnover for a category. Periodically run an inventory turnover report by category and note how many categories are at the edges of the range. You may want to alter your buying plan to carry more of the productive items.

Each item should be tracked long enough to determine how it usually sells, or you can initially rely on industry standards. If the previous period represents how the item performs on a regular basis, then you have sufficient information to come to some conclusions. If it was unusually slow or busy, the sales results will cause you to overestimate or underestimate sales performance over a longer period of time.

Turnover information is especially useful as it pertains to category of merchandise. You might be buying too many pieces and hurting your overall sales. Simply by narrowing your assortment, you might significantly improve your turnover and thereby get a better return on your investment.

In some instances, you might want to stock an item even though the turnover is consistently and predictably low. Books, products aimed at a specific narrow audience, and high-end products that are a good fit with your museum's mission are examples. These items might not be bestsellers, but they may attract a different segment of visitors, improve the image of your store, or further the museum's educational goals.

It is important to note that too high a turnover rate can result in diminishing benefit. The higher the rate of turnover, the more ordering; the higher the freight charges, the more receiving, pricing, and merchandising needs to be done. The cost in terms of time and staffing to keep up with a high rate of turnover might eliminate any positive effects. Often the first products to be out of stock because of high turnover are the most popular products. Customer disappointment and the loss of a disproportionate amount of sales are the result of this condition.

MANAGING YOUR INVENTORY AND INVENTORY COUNTS

INVENTORY MANAGEMENT

If your store generates more than about $25,000 per year in revenue, you should be using POS system software. These can range from inexpensive and simple systems such as Shopify or Square to an array of more robust and sophisticated products. These systems, with their perpetual inventory, purchase-order creation, accounting, report generating, price tag printing, receiving, and other modules, are the single most effective tool for inventory management. A POS system shows you exactly where your inventory is—or should be—and gives you the tools and knowledge to react. For more on POS systems, refer to chapter 3.

Pay close attention to inventory results in

- increased inventory turns with fewer dollars invested in inventory at any one time,
- better cash flow,
- fresher product selection,
- the ability to quickly react to new products,
- fewer markdowns, and
- fewer "trapped" items lost in back stock.

Maintaining adequate stock requires a periodic review of inventory. Most retailers rely on several types of inventory control:

- Periodic: Using either a visual or written record, inventory is reviewed on a fixed basis.
- Perpetual: Written records track every purchase on a daily basis. Depletion is then compared with stock records.
- Cycle counts: Taking physical inventory of a single item or category on a scheduled, ongoing basis.

For tax and insurance purposes as well as to gauge a store's profitability, a physical inventory must be taken at least once a year. Accurate counting of the stock helps to

- determine the store's assets,
- assess buying patterns,
- reduce shrinkage,
- familiarize yourself with the stock on hand,
- identify and limit wasteful purchases,
- quickly identify slow sellers, and
- identify shortages and employ proper recourse.

Overstocking saddles a retailer with several hidden costs, including the following:

- Carrying costs: Storage, insurance, overhead.
- Cost of committed funds: Money tied up in inventory.
- Opportunity cost: Funds tied up in inventory can't be used on new and perhaps more salable products.

It is especially important to keep track of your bestselling products. Typically, 60 percent to 70 percent of your revenue is generated by about 30 percent of your product. So if you are out of your bestselling products, you're not just out of a product, you are out of a product that generates a high percentage of sales and customer satisfaction.

Many experts recommend that small retailers consider more frequent inventories. The best rule, however, is to take full or spot inventories as often as needed to keep on top of your inventory status and selling patterns. Smaller retailers can't absorb the losses that result from untended problems, such as theft or pervasive damages.

VALUATION METHODS

Retailers generally rely on one of two systems of valuation for physical inventories:

- The retail method, which values each unit at its selling price.
- The cost method, which values each unit of merchandise at its original cost.

Retail valuation at cost can be a more stable number because it reflects actual cost to the institution to acquire the inventory and the current financial liability on the balance sheet and it does not vary by pricing strategy, markups, or future markdowns.

Recording open inventory at both cost and retail allows you to determine a markup percentage. It also provides a mechanism for analyzing and comparing the profitability of various departments.

UNIT CONTROL

If a physical inventory is to be meaningful, you must have a reliable system of unit control that lists the number of units carried over from previous inventories as well as those received, sold, and on hand during a specified period. The sum of units sold and those on hand should equal the sum of the units received and the units carried over. If your unit control system is adequate, the stock on hand should correspond to the findings of a physical inventory.

INVENTORY FORMS

With the unit control system in place, you are ready to take a physical inventory. The first step is to obtain the appropriate forms. Many office supply stores stock inventory forms, or retailers can design their own.

All inventories begin with a map of the physical areas to be counted. Staff are assigned to areas for accountability. Mapping is an effective tool in count organization and efficiency in identifying recount and error areas. Your inventory control (IC) system will allow you to count by scanning each product; the system then records the count. Audits are recommended to be sure that each piece is scanned. When completed, your system will print a variance report that checks the physical scanned count against the book amount in your record.

The manual form should record the date of the inventory and the names of the persons involved in the counting. The form should also include several vertical columns with the following headers:

- Description of item
- SKU/barcode
- If applicable, the classification or category under which the merchandise falls, for example, decorative items, books, paper products, apparel
- Number of units
- Retail price per unit
- Total value of units (to be totaled at the bottom of the page)

Your count includes merchandise in the warehouse, stockroom, fixture storage, and will-call or hold sections and that are displayed in the store.

INVENTORY PROCEDURES

Taking inventory requires the planning and cooperation of each member of a store's staff. You may hire an outside service to count and record or use your staff. Either way, controls must be in place. When planning an inventory, consider the following:

- If possible, do not take the inventory over several days; complete it in one session. The store must be closed and shipping and receiving stopped.
- Number your inventory forms and distribute them to assigned staff. Make sure all the sheets are returned.
- Give all participants uniform written instructions and training and provide them with a map or list of areas they are to inventory.
- Allow for periodic spot checks as inventory sheets are filled out and plan to check at least 25 percent of the sheets against inventory.

- Make sure your inventory does not include new merchandise yet to be entered into the books. Establish a cutoff date after which you will not receive inventory into stock.
- Take inventory as close to the end of the calendar or fiscal year as possible.

The results of the inventory are compared with the totals in your inventory records. If the physical count reveals that you have more merchandise on hand than a book inventory indicates, you have a stock overage. Less merchandise means a stock shortage. Bear in mind that overages and shortages could be the result of counting errors. In either case, attempts should be made to reconcile or explain the differences.

TRACKING SHRINKAGE

Under ideal circumstances, your physical inventory will match your book inventory. All too often, however, inventories reveal a stock shortage.

Shortages, also known as stock shrinkage, increase the cost of goods sold and shrink net profits. The most common causes of shortages, in descending order of frequency, are

- customer shoplifting;
- employee theft; and
- inaccurate record keeping, including the following:
  - unnoticed shipping errors,
  - incorrect counts,
  - misassigned SKUs,
  - broken and damaged goods not removed from inventory, and
  - donated items not removed from inventory.

Although some shrinkage is inevitable, it pays to ensure that your store does not exceed industry norms. These are tricky to calculate. In a typical museum store setting, you should be concerned about shrinkage that is more than 1.5 percent of net sales. Combating shrinkage involves everything from overhauling your books to preventing theft.

Follow this formula to calculate shrinkage:

Book* Inventory − Physical Inventory = Inventory Variance

(*Inventory count derived from receiving kept in your IC system)

Inventory shortage ÷ Net Sales × 100 = Inventory
Shortage as a Percentage of Net Sales

SUMMARY POINTS

- Your merchandising plan is a useful tool for meeting a sales plan and adjusting to promotional efforts.
- Using an OTB system allows management to meet sales demands with a minimum of shortages and without excessive inventory levels.
- The museum's mission and your customer profile should guide your buying and product development decisions.
- Become educated about copyright law before embarking on a licensing program.
- Tracking inventory can improve a store's bottom line through better product selection and increased inventory turns.

5

Store Layout, Design, and Displays

Chapter Highlights

- Strategically planning the store layout
- Designing displays with accessibility in mind
- Store design
- Signage
- Other factors
- Merchandising for maximum impact

A well-designed museum store should align with the museum's mission, cater to the specific needs and preferences of its diverse visitors, and tell a compelling narrative. Before delving into the intricate details of design and merchandise display, it's imperative to lay a strong foundation by answering three fundamental questions about your museum store: Who are the visitors? What do they buy? And, perhaps most importantly, what is your story?

STRATEGICALLY PLANNING THE STORE LAYOUT

Because there are so many different kinds of museums attracting a wide variety of visitors to retail settings of varying sizes and locations, there can't truly be absolute store design and display criteria. However, there are key factors to consider when remodeling an existing store or designing a new store.

A successful museum store layout does the following:

- Entices visitors to enter the store. This may sound elementary, but if they don't come in, they can't buy. Make their first view interesting, exciting, and compelling! Use attractive displays and graphics to attract a visitor's attention. Arrange fixtures to encourage easy traffic flow and not cause overcrowding. The challenge: People like to see a busy store (an empty one can be intimidating) but not one so crowded that they won't be able to see everything and that have long checkout lines.

  All other factors being equal, the best location for the store is on the right side as the visitor approaches the exit from the museum. Ideally, the store should be visible from the museum's entrance and very prominent at the exit. The first thing visitors see should be attractive and in harmony with the tenor of the museum.

- Moves people throughout the store. The storefront should give visitors a feel for the store before they enter it. Wide, open entrances or double-width doors are more inviting than narrow or constricted entrances. This is especially important when the museum is busy so that visitors do not feel the store is too crowded to enter.

  Significant ebbs and flows of visitors are a fact of life in a museum store, especially when the museum is busy, so customers must be encouraged to browse throughout the store.

- Inspires visitors to linger. This is an important goal of store design and layout because the longer people stay in the store, the better the chance they will find something of interest to buy.

- Increases the average transaction. Because return visits to museum stores are less frequent than to commercial stores, it is critical to create an atmosphere that encourages purchases now.

- Creates sight lines that improve customer service and discourage shoplifting. Although staff training is the most important factor in this area, the layout needs to facilitate these activities.

- Enhances the overall image of the museum. The store is usually one of the last and lasting impressions of the museum, so everything in the store should validate the impression the museum wants to make on the visitor.

GENERAL LAYOUT

Stores generally are designed according to one of two layout schemes. The grid layout positions display racks and aisles according to geometric patterns, and customers generally pass up and down aisles before returning to the entrance and the cash register. The freeform layout offers no direct path and allows customers to wander according to whim with aisles leading around displays or cutting across the store in a diagonal.

Although the grid layout is less pleasing to the eye than the freeform layout, it often works best for stores with limited floor space. Small stores generally need to channel traffic to avoid jams and confusion.

The freeform layout is ideal for spacious stores that can accommodate unstructured traffic flow. Although few museum stores have dressing rooms, they generally are located toward the rear of the store and, most importantly, should have lighting that enhances the appearance of the apparel—and the customer. It is best to display items such as books, near which customers tend to converge and linger, in the back of the store so they don't block people from entering the store.

DESIGNING DISPLAYS WITH ACCESSIBILITY IN MIND

Make sure your fixtures allow space for comfortable passage of wheelchair users. The thirty-six-inch clearance required by the Americans with Disabilities Act (ADA) is often not enough to allow shoppers who use wheelchairs to browse and turn. Evaluate your store, considering the perspective of guests who use a variety of mobility devices (wheelchairs, walkers, canes, crutches) to locate areas in need of improvement. Look at floor surfaces, shelf height, counters (especially at the cash wrap), kiosks, and pathways to ensure that all customers can reach your products easily. Keep passageways unobstructed and merchandise products in a way that makes them easy to see, reach, and pick up.

Maintain a balance between aesthetics and functionality, using legible fonts and high-contrast colors to enhance readability for those with visual impairments, such as color blindness. Make sure that the displays are well lit to aid visitors with low vision and consider offering magnifying tools or assistive devices upon request. Many generally good visual merchandising practices also make your store easier to access both visually and physically. Universal design factors benefit all museum guests.

STORE DESIGN

The following factors are important to successful layout and design. The store design is important for both sales and looks. In a museum setting a significant percentage of customers don't know what to expect from the store, so most buying decisions are made on the floor at the time of the visit.

DISPLAY WINDOW

The purpose of display windows, whether they face the museum interior or the street, should be to entice the visitor to cross the threshold into the store. Large, simple displays focused on the exhibits in the museum are usually the most appropriate. Because the typical visitor does not know what to expect from the store, the display window should offer a glimpse of what the store has to offer.

FLOOR COVERING

At the entrance(s), the floor should be easy to clean. These are high-traffic areas and should be durable and practical for cleaning and replacement. Factors to consider include the following:

- Durability
- Ease of maintenance
- Cost

Inside the store, changes in floor surfaces can do the following:

- Set off product
- Lead customers
- Stimulate interest
- Differentiate departments
- Encourage lingering (for example, people stand longer in front of books and jewelry displays)
- Enhance the ambiance of higher-priced or more sophisticated products

COLOR

The merchandise should be the star, and color selection should enhance the appearance of the merchandise. You might want to create a color chart that specifies acceptable shades, tones, and colors. For example, if your store design calls to mind a Victorian parlor, forgo bright primary colors.

Color compatibility is especially important when displaying multicolored items. Accent colors can then be used as needed but should not compete with the product. Good color opportunities include graphics; floor coverings; and fixture facings, finishes, and detailing. In general, the larger the fixture, the lighter and more neutral the color should be.

FIXTURES

Fixtures should be designed to showcase merchandise in an attractive and easily accessible manner. Buying is a tactile experience: the more the customers' senses are stimulated, the more they are likely to buy. When customers can't directly access products, staff must provide sufficient and attentive customer service.

Fixtures can also be efficient tools for store management. They should be flexible, including a combination of adjustable shelves, slat wall backs, and casters. Flexible fixtures result in a better return on investment and are easier for staff to work with when changing displays.

The first fixture in the store should be close enough to the entrance to attract customers but back far enough to draw them across the threshold into the shop. The height of fixtures should increase toward the back and on perimeter walls, drawing customers in and allowing them to see as much of the store as possible. Fixtures should never be more imposing than the products they display.

BACK WALL

The far reaches of the store should be treated like the tallest fixture in the store and should be one of the brightest lit areas of the store. Larger, brighter colored, and easily recognizable products merchandised in this area will act as a magnet to draw customers from the front third of the store through to the rear.

CHECKOUT

The checkout counter is a delicate balance of service, display, and security, and it creates a lasting impression of the store and museum. The primary purposes of the checkout counter are the following:

- Serve as a focal point for customer service (although it is far better to have this happen on the floor).
- Display impulse items that customers may pick up when they are waiting or involved in their sales transaction. If the sales desk is designed to also display jewelry items, keep it clear of clutter and have staff available to assist a customer at all times.
- Offer an opportunity to thank customers for their purchases and leave them with a positive impression of the entire visit to the museum.

An ancillary purpose is to sell more merchandise. It is an ideal location to display impulse merchandise that increases the average purchase, but it should be kept uncluttered. Sales transactions should be handled quickly and efficiently. The longer people wait at the checkout counter, the lower their perception of the overall service in the store.

Strong customer service and eye contact are the most significant factors affecting the level of shoplifting. Whereas the checkout counter should probably not be at the rear of the store, it should not be at the very front. If the staff is trained to make eye contact, be out on the floor (not huddled behind the register), and provide adequate attention to customer service, there is more flexibility in the location of the counter. Also bear in mind that the sales counter can cause congestion, so location and line control is important.

LIGHTING

Lighting experts and retail managers agree that lighting can have a positive effect on sales, and poor lighting hurts profits. Modern lighting technology offers a variety of environmentally safe, cost-effective ways to brightly highlight or softly accent merchandise in your store.

This is one area in which you should spend the money to engage an expert because the rewards of effective lighting can be significant. The key purpose of lighting is to manipulate the customer's attention. There are three primary light sources:

- Fluorescent lighting is economical and energy efficient, it comes in a wide variety of colors, and it is most commonly used in general and perimeter applications. Compact fluorescent lights (CFLs) are fine for lamps.
- Light-emitting diodes (LEDs) are more costly up front, but their long life makes them a bargain. They can provide well-defined beams that are useful in accent lighting.
- Spotlighting is used for illuminating designated displays, whereas ambient lighting washes a room with indirect light. A combination works well. Track lighting affords maximum flexibility in using both kinds of lights and aiming them accurately.

Maintain a balance in the type and number of light fixtures used throughout a store. The following are good choices for specific display applications:

- Plenty of light directed to bookcases.
- Compact linear lighting that is easily concealed inside a display case.
- Economical, long-lasting halogen spotlights are good for highlighting.
- Well-placed track lighting illuminates areas of special interest.

What type of lighting does your museum use in spaces? Keep this in mind to extend the tone and style of the institution into the museum store.

Achieving just the right amount of illumination for different areas of your store requires continual experimentation. Here are some general rules to follow:

- Self-service showcases should be brighter than service showcases.
- Jewelry cases need an amount of light twice as bright as the ambient light in the store. Be sure that there is enough ventilation in closed cases so the heat does not damage the items on display.
- Lighting in aisles and circulation areas need not be as high as in other areas; this setup helps call attention to brighter display areas.
- Transaction areas and areas deeper into the store need more light.
- There is a strong preference by customers for warm, bright lighting. Lighting has evolved to long-life, energy-efficient, and cool-temperature options that are more comfortable for the customers and create less damage to products.

SECURITY

The layout and lighting of your store should inhibit shoplifting. Be sure to consider the following:

- Locate the main sales desk in a spot that affords a view of the entire store.
- Avoid use of tall partitions that block any area from view: keep sight lines open.
- Position hands-on display cases in full view of the sales desk.
- Keep all hands-on cases fully illuminated.
- Display valuable items in locked, glass-front cases.
- Place as many fixtures as possible perpendicular to the checkout counter and the perimeter walls to reduce the number of customers who have their backs to the primary service area.

SIGNAGE

EXTERIOR SIGNAGE

Unless the predominant flow of visitor traffic is straight toward the entrance to the store, it is important to have exterior signage perpendicular to the flow of foot traffic. Directional signage to the store should be placed at key locations within the museum, including the following:

- The museum entrance
- Exits from permanent/special exhibitions
- High-traffic areas, such as food service sites, restrooms, and coat check

STORE GRAPHICS AND INTERIOR SIGNAGE

A good sign acts as a silent salesperson: never absent, always accurate and timely. Signs communicate more than what is written on them by being professional-looking, consistent, usually brief, and placed in advantageous locations. Be sure that the point size of the type can be read several feet away. Signs should stand out but not overpower the merchandise. The size of your signs can vary, the messages can vary, but the color, font, and style should remain consistent throughout the store and relate to the institution's overall image.

With modern digital signage, stores can now update sign information to ensure it is up to date without wasting paper. Some digital displays can showcase more than just information; they can be a rich addition by adding images and videos to your shelves. Bring a behind-the-scenes video of an artisan's process to your customers, demonstrate a product, or share how it connects to your latest exhibition. Digital displays can add variety to your displays.

Signage is most effective when the following are incorporated into the design:

- Clean, simple, and eye-catching look
- Minimal text
- Brevity and pointedness
- Price-point signage that matches the merchandise price ticket
- No more than two or three colors; be sure not to combine unreadable colors (yellow is almost never an easy read for text; white letters on pale anything is difficult as well)
- Light letters on a dark background or dark letters on a light background for readability
- Legible fonts that are simple and large enough to read
- Images that are part of the sign, not the focal point

Certain merchandise requires special attention. Here are some more specific suggestions:

- Books should be arranged by subject with sections identified for children.
- Apparel should be clearly identified by type and size.
- Children's toys and games can be categorized by age.
- Small information cards provide a critical link to the objects in the collection that the products represent and the educational mission of the store.
- Products developed directly from the museum's collections should be identified.
- Special services should be highlighted:

  - "We ship anything anywhere" signs near heavy or fragile merchandise and at the checkout counter might remove the objection to buying one or more of these products.
  - Gift wrapping and willingness to place special orders promote the service-oriented aspect of your store's customer care program.
  - There should be no negative signage in your store. Say "We're happy to assist you" instead of "Don't touch."

OTHER FACTORS

MUSIC

Today most customers use music streaming services, so selling CDs is no longer practical. Some streaming services offer nonprofit discounts or tiered accounts that are reasonably priced to use in a museum. You can collaborate with other museum departments to choose a tiered account that fits all your needs and provides background music to the public areas of the museum without running afoul of licensing laws. Choose music that appeals to the customers, not the employees. If you have background music, position speakers throughout the store if possible to avoid loud spots.

SCENTS

Be aware of strong scents:

- Many customers have allergies that will drive them from your store if it is heavily scented.
- Heavy scents have a negative effect on many customers who simply don't like them.
- Merchandise heavily scented products toward the rear of the store to give the ventilation system an opportunity to dissipate the scent before it reaches the entrance.

SEATING

If you're considering offering seating, keep the following in mind:

- The tradeoff is longer lingering versus less merchandisable space: weigh the value of this real estate.
- Older customers appreciate seating.
- It gives the person who is less interested in the buying experience a place to sit down while a more motivated buyer shops.

MERCHANDISING FOR MAXIMUM IMPACT

Where and how the product is placed in the store makes a difference in how customers view it. The following are some points to consider:

- The density of merchandising and height of fixtures should increase as you move into the store and off the main walkways.
- A product that requires extensive customer attention should not be near the front or on the first fixture because it can cause traffic jams.
- More sophisticated products should be merchandised toward the back where the foot traffic is less and a thoughtful ambiance for the product can more easily be established. (The more customers have to evaluate a product, the more they need a "quiet" space around them.)
- Designate a focused display space for products that pertain to a temporary exhibition and use signs to call attention to it.
- Children's items should be grouped together, away from expensive adult items, and displayed at a level that can be seen.
- Adjacent placement of products is important: group complementary items together.
- Place high-margin items at eye level.

- Place high-volume items slightly above or below eye level.
- Nobody shops below their knees.
- Merchandise vertically first, then horizontally as it is easier for customers to stand still and look up and down to take in a product category than to move their feet.
- Customers have a very strong tendency to go to their right, so facilitating this natural tendency will benefit sales.
- Impulse (high-volume, high-margin) items should be close to the checkout counter.

The front third of your store gets a disproportionate percentage of foot traffic and, often, sales. Display new products, higher-margin items, and things you want to make sure the customer sees to the right toward the front of the store.

DESIGNING AN EFFECTIVE VISUAL DISPLAY

Visual presentation is an integral component of a merchandising plan. It includes creative display, awareness of lighting and display options, display standards, and wise use of information cards. Most customers don't buy products out of need but rather out of impulse. Artful presentation can stimulate a customer's desire for a product.

Displays are particularly important in museum stores because typical customers have already spent time looking at exhibits and their eyes have become trained to artful presentation. They might be too tired or short on time to take in the entire store, product by product. An effective display focuses customers' attention on smaller numbers of select products that you want to make sure they see.

The first rule of creative presentation is that anything goes—anything, that is, except clutter and sloppiness. Be different, but with a purpose. Effective displays lengthen lingering and increase the average transaction. Every display should be neat, clean, and uncluttered.

Displays should be changed frequently: at least once a month for stores with primarily a tourist clientele and twice a month for those that enjoy repeat customers.

When evaluating your display options, remember these key points:

- Vendors often supply free display fixtures designed specifically to enhance the products you have purchased. (Take advantage of these only when the fixtures are consistent with the ambiance of your store.)
- Customers appreciate a few tips on using the product, which can be implied through a display.
- Displays with a theme are more interesting to customers than a seemingly random grouping of products.

Display themes can include the following:

- What's new: A consistent display of the newest products will be especially popular with your repeat customers and the large segment of your customers who like to be the first on the block to have anything new.
- Suggestions: Show customers how a piece of pottery could be used in their homes or how a group of prints might be framed and hung.
- Add-ons: Display ancillary and enhancing products together to suggest combinations of multiple products.
- Slow-moving items: Focus attention on slow-moving items, and more of them will be sold at full price.
- Temporary: Exhibition-related, special event, and seasonal items.

EXPERIENCE RETAILING

Museum stores are one of the earliest examples of experience retailing in its simplest form. The shops are built off of permanent and special exhibitions. Simple techniques, such as color schemes featured in exhibitions, can be recreated in the retail area, extending the museum experience into the store. Other ideas include the following:

- Reproductions of the more prominent exhibition items and key images that create the feeling that the museum tour continues into the store.
- Clever signage that piques visitors' curiosity and leads them to merchandise with questions such as, "Do you want to know more about . . . ?"
- Use of information cards that tie merchandise to the museum experience.
- Appropriate merchandise and adequate stock that helps you capitalize on seasonal and topical trends.

ARTFUL PRESENTATION

One of the simplest ways of displaying merchandise is to group it with aesthetically compatible products: jewel-toned scarves with gemstone bracelets or Chinese vases with jade figurines. Often a book on the subject of the merchandise can round out a strong display. Another way is to enhance the merchandise with carefully selected props. Props can encompass everything from dried flowers to model airplanes or anything that, when combined with the merchandise, tells a story or paints a picture. Be aware that any prop is taking the place of a product that can be sold and use them sparingly.

Book purchases can be inspired by a customer's visit to an exhibition with a captivating title or an intriguing image adorning a book's jacket. Books sell more quickly face out than spine out as customers are more likely to pick up a book based on the cover than the title. If you want to keep multiple copies on the sales floor, place several spine out and then one or multiples face out. Books have their own set of challenges; for one thing, they are all basically the same shape. Use the graphic quality of the covers to break up the monotony and create points of interest. Sometimes placing a related product in the bookcase has a dramatic effect. Don't place books out of reach of the customer. If you have tall bookcases, consider displaying extra stock of prints or other products on these shelves (but be sure you have those displayed elsewhere in the store within reach). You can use this to tell a story. A print of a painting and a paint kit can be displayed above or among the art books.

Small, cleverly placed displays can be decision makers. They draw shoppers to an area of the store by highlighting a few well-chosen, representative products. Effective displays boost sales by

- grabbing a customer's attention,
- offering easy access to merchandise conveniently stocked nearby, and
- providing cross-merchandising opportunities that expand potential sales.

When grouping merchandise or showcasing it with a prop, consider the following:

- Small groupings of odd numbers are especially eye catching.
- If customers ask to buy the props, you've gone too far.
- Each cluster of merchandise should have a focal point.
- Display case linings should not clash with the merchandise or with the store's flooring. Avoid printed fabrics. These often detract from the merchandise.
- When one item from the display is sold, replace it immediately or rearrange the display.
- Make sure all price tags are consistent in appearance and positioning.
- Display tall items in the back or use risers to elevate products. Put shorter items in front. This gives optimum viewing to all merchandise in the display.
- Put signs where they are easily read.
- Repetition is an effective technique for visual impact. (Whereas one or two of an item might not be eye catching, ten or twenty neatly displayed identical items make a statement.)

In display cases, keep in mind:

- The pyramid technique works best for items in multishelf display cases.
- The top shelf should have the least amount of merchandise.
- The bottom shelf should have the most merchandise.

When working with displays of colorful items, follow basic visual merchandising concepts related to eye movement:

- Arrange light colors on the left; place darker colors on the right.
- Placing a vibrantly colorful product in the middle of more subdued tones can highlight the colorful product and invite closer scrutiny of the paler ones.

Take note of display ideas you see in other stores, magazines, and online retail stores or visual merchandising sites.

SUMMARY POINTS

- Store design is important for both the sales and the visual impact.
- Display new products and high-margin items in the front third of the store where foot traffic is highest.
- Product displays should be neat, clean, and uncluttered.

6

Managing Staff

Chapter Highlights

- Leadership words of wisdom
- Working with your museum's union
- DEAI in the workplace
- Selecting staff and establishing personnel policies
- Training and managing staff
- Recruiting and managing volunteers
- Consultants

LEADERSHIP WORDS OF WISDOM

The following is a collection of wise words from colleagues and professionals:

- Listen, learn, lead.
- Be respectful, be fair.
- Improve on what you can.
- Be clear in your expectations.
- Applaud.
- Practice active listening.
- Manage by example.
- Own it.
- Coach your staff like you would like to be coached.
- Trust and delegate.
- Always have your organization's interests at heart.

- Learn what you don't know and teach what you do know.
- Your team is not a social club: focus on deliverables.
- Manage by walking: don't stay in the office.
- You may have the title, but your team controls your future.

As a manager, one of your most important jobs is selecting, training, motivating, and directing employees. Frontline staff are the public face of your organization. If you take care of your staff, they will take care of your customers, and the customers, in return, will support your business.

WORKING WITH YOUR MUSEUM'S UNION

It is important to recognize that, if your museum's staff operates under union agreements, not all advice and best practices that follow in this chapter will apply.

For museum store managers, it's crucial to work with your human resources (HR) department to understand and familiarize yourself with the collective bargaining agreement (CBA) that governs the terms and conditions of employment of your institution's unionized staff. HR professionals can provide valuable guidance on how to align your museum store's operations with the CBA, ensuring compliance and fairness.

Working with unionized staff does not need to be adversarial; in fact, it can be a collaborative partnership. Instead of reserving interactions with union representatives, members, and staff solely for tense situations, cultivate positive relationships. Maintain open, transparent lines of communication, ensuring that both the union and HR are kept informed of any changes that may impact staff. Transparency builds trust and facilitates smoother collaboration.

Laws and regulations regarding unionized workplaces can change, and CBAs can be renegotiated. Stay current on labor laws and regulations, ensuring that your store's practices remain compliant with the current CBA.

By staying informed, museum store managers can successfully navigate the union environment.

DEAI IN THE WORKPLACE

In no area are DEAI principles more important than in the hiring and managing of the teams who make your museum function from day to day.

A diverse team is not only better equipped to meet the evolving needs of a diverse museum audience, but it also fosters creativity, innovation, and a deeper connection with the communities served. By fostering inclusivity in staffing and museum practices, we pave the way for a richer, more engaging, and respectful workplace.

Challenge biases in hiring and management by developing a critical lens for evaluating your hiring and management processes and ask crucial questions, such as, "In what ways are our hiring and management practices supporting racist, classist, ableist, and heteronormative norms prevalent in the museum community?" Discover strategies for mitigating these biases and fostering equitable opportunities for all.

As a manager, it is important to have a comprehensive understanding of diversity, acknowledging its multifaceted aspects, including age, race, gender identities, religions, cultural backgrounds, physical abilities, and neurodiversity. Appreciate how these elements contribute to the richness of museum experiences and the needs of your audience.

Accommodations are critical for staff members with physical needs and neurodivergence. Work with your HR department to enable effective strategies for providing the support and adjustments necessary to ensure an inclusive work environment.

Consider the significance of supporting time off needs, particularly during major holidays of religions that may not align with national holidays. Learn how to create a work culture that respects the religious and cultural diversity of your team.

Keep each of these concepts in mind when selecting staff, working with staff, and developing your budget.

SELECTING STAFF AND ESTABLISHING PERSONNEL POLICIES

Hiring the right people for your store requires a clear sense of what you want and a fair amount of perseverance. The hiring process for museum jobs has often been fraught with gatekeeping and discrimination, so make sure that your process is equitable and that you think clearly about your present needs rather than following old practices that may have fallen out of date.

The first steps are to write a clear job description and then a job posting based on that. A good ad for a job is aimed at attracting your ideal candidate. Use the job description to compose a series of questions to ask each applicant in an interview. It is helpful to assign scoring to each question based on importance. Add a space for personalized notes. Be fair and expressive, but be careful what you write in the notes. If there are ever any legal issues about the applicant, employee, or you, these notes are discoverable.

JOB DESCRIPTIONS

Make your job descriptions clear and specific. List the duties of the job on which the employee will be evaluated. Prioritize the use of gender-neutral and universally understood language. Carefully consider the education, skills, and experience you are asking for. For example, is a college degree truly a qualification for work on your team, or is that listed on the template for all museum job descriptions out of long-held tradition? Do you require previous work experience in a museum environment, or would equivalent experience in the commercial retail or hospitality sector easily transfer? Read your job description thinking about your enterprise from the perspectives of different prospective candidates from a range of different backgrounds and abilities: What language might be unin-tentionally discriminatory toward fully qualified candidates?

To avoid confusion, duplication of effort, and inefficiency, it's wise to keep written job descriptions for each staff member, including yourself. Job descrip-tions should include the following:

- A general description of the position
- Notation of whether the job is part or full time, temporary or permanent
- A list of any superiors to whom the employee reports
- A statement of all specific duties and key outcomes
- Physical requirements, such as the amount of weight that must be lifted; length of time standing; ability to bend and kneel, work outside, etc.; check with HR for state and federal regulations

JOB POSTINGS

To ensure equitable and inclusive job postings, organizations should do the following:

- Provide transparent salary information.
- Use clear job titles and descriptions.
- Simplify the application process.
- Advertise in various channels and platforms that target a broad range of candidates (such as school job boards, LinkedIn, Indeed, and on the museum site).
- Ensure job postings are accessible to all. This includes making sure that they are compatible with screen readers and that any videos or images are accompanied by descriptive text.

INTERVIEW QUESTIONS

Keep your interviews as standardized as possible so that each candidate has the same time and context in which to present their qualifications. Write your questions in advance. Open-ended and experiential questions ("Tell me about a time when you . . .") are good as they allow candidates to give you a view of how they approach their work.

INTERVIEW PROCESS

Now you are ready to begin interviewing. Match the résumés as closely as possible to your job description and conduct phone screens with those who are most qualified. It is helpful to have a scored list of questions that are a bit broader than face-to-face interview questions. The phone screen acts as a quick interview to decide which candidates have the basic skills and require-ments to move on to the next steps. Narrow the number of candidates to your top two or three and invite them for in-person or virtual interviews.

An interview is a two-way conversation. Do not spend all your time talking about your organization or about you. Be brief initially so you are not feeding answers to the candidate. Don't fill every silent moment: let the candidate do that. Stay away from yes or no questions. Give candidates the opportunity to show you what they bring to the table. Leave time at the end for them to ask you questions. Don't forget that not only are candidates selling their skills, you are selling the organization and the job to them. Before making a final decision, check a candidate's references.

Before interviewing:

- It's important to familiarize yourself with state and federal opportunity and discrimination laws.
- Ask the candidates the same basic set of questions and rank them for importance. This way, you have a common basis to use when making decisions.
- Prepare questions designed to discover whether the candidate exhibits these qualities.
- List, in order of importance, the skills the employee should have.
- If there are required technical skills (writing, systems expertise, etc.), prepare proficiency tests for the applicants to complete.

OVERCOMING OUTDATED INTERVIEW PRACTICES

Relying on subjective assessments such as "Will the candidate get along with other personnel?" and "Will supervisors feel comfortable with the candidate?" can hinder diversity and perpetuate biases.

To create a more equitable hiring process, consider the following:

- Structured interviewing:
  - Implement a structured interview process that focuses on specific job-related competencies and skills, like the Sample Candidate Scorecard. By using a set of standardized questions for all candidates, you create a fair and consistent evaluation framework that minimizes the impact of personal biases.

- Behavioral interviewing:
  - Because you are hiring people who will interface with the public and likely be the last experience a visitor has at the museum, you want to conduct a behavioral interview to determine how they handle various situations. This information cannot be gleaned from asking questions with yes or no answers. Prepare questions asking the candidate to deal with hypothetical situations: Describe a time when. . . . And how did you respond? These provide insight into the candidate's resourcefulness, composure, and common sense.

CANDIDATE SCORECARD

CANDIDATE NAME:	POSITION:
INTERVIEWER/S:	DATE:

SCORING

Candidate evaluation forms are to be completed by the interviewer to rank the candidate's overall qualifications for the position to which he or she has applied. Under each heading, the interviewer should give the candidate a numerical rating and write specific job-related comments in the space provided. The numerical rating system is based on the following:

5 - Exceptional **4** - Above Average **3** - Average **2** - Below Average **1** - Unsatisfactory

Educational Background: Does the candidate have the appropriate educational qualifications or training for this position?	**RATING:**				
	5	4	3	2	1

Comments:

Prior Work Experience: Has the candidate acquired similar skills or qualifications through past work experiences?	**RATING:**				
	5	4	3	2	1

Comments:

Technical Qualifications/Experience: Does the candidate have the technical skills necessary for this position?	**RATING:**				
	5	4	3	2	1

Comments:

Verbal Communication: Did the candidate demonstrate effective communication skills during the interview?	**RATING:**				
	5	4	3	2	1

Comments:

Candidate Enthusiasm: Did the candidate show enthusiasm for the position and the company?	**RATING:**				
	5	4	3	2	1

Comments:

Figure 6.1.   Candidate Scorecard. *The Museum Store Association*

Knowledge of Company: Did the candidate show evidence of having researched the company prior to the interview?	RATING:				
	5	4	3	2	1

Comments:

Teambuilding/Interpersonal Skills: Did the candidate demonstrate, through his or her answers, good teambuilding/interpersonal skills?	RATING:				
	5	4	3	2	1

Comments:

Initiative: Did the candidate demonstrate, through his or her answers, a high degree of initiative?	RATING:				
	5	4	3	2	1

Comments:

Time Management: Did the candidate demonstrate, through his or her answers, good time management skills?	RATING:				
	5	4	3	2	1

Comments:

Customer Service: Did the candidate demonstrate, through his or her answers, a high level of customer service skills/abilities?	RATING:				
	5	4	3	2	

Comments:

Overall Impression and Recommendation: Final comments and recommendations for proceeding with the candidate.	RATING:				
	5	4	3	2	

Comments:

TOTAL:					

ONBOARDING

Once you have made a decision and your offer for the position has been accepted, it's critical to have a good plan for bringing new employees on board. Employees with good onboarding experiences stay longer and are more confident in their jobs.

Whether you are managing a small or large staff, paid or volunteer, it's wise to prepare a written policy outlining your expectations of all personnel. Written policies allow you to be consistent in everything from awarding raises to allocating vacation time. Such a policy should describe the standards you expect employees to uphold as well as any repercussions should they fail to do so. As personnel matters are subject to litigation, it's vital for the museum's legal counsel and HR experts to review all policies carefully. The following list, although not complete and comprehensive, contains several important policy issues:

- Work hours
- Timetable for evaluations and raises
- Type of raises: merit or cost of living
- Benefits: health insurance, paid vacations, personal days, sick leave, 401(k), pension, etc.

Outline standards and policies regarding the following:

- Personal, family, maternity, paternity leave
- Dress guidelines
- Employee discounts
- Pay schedule
- Procedures for resignation
- Absenteeism
- Substance abuse
- Theft
- Sexual harassment
- Discrimination
- Causes and procedures for dismissal

To promote equity and fairness within your organization, there must be transparent policies for management. Well-defined guidelines addressing topics such as nepotism, conflict of interest, and promotion proactively address ethical dilemmas, ensuring a just and ethical workplace environment.

It is important to adhere to your own policies and to treat each employee consistently. Inconsistent behavior on your part undermines employees' respect for you and erodes morale. It's crucial that you follow as well as make rules. You can expect personnel to follow the example you set.

As you present the rules to your staff, be sure to present the positive nature of communication and collaboration:

- Don't assume employees are happy: create a safe feedback environment.
- Hold regular meetings and have a method for expression of ideas and suggestions.
- Allow staff to participate in reaching departmental goals.
- Don't hold information as currency: share appropriately and enthusiastically.

ORIENTATION

After hiring a new employee, you need to introduce the employee to your business. A general orientation includes the following:

- An introduction to the institution's mission statement and statement of purpose.
- A tour of the museum to encourage familiarity with the exhibits.
- A tour of the store as well as of the stockroom and office.
- An introduction to all other staff members.
- An explanation of employee policies and store procedures.
- A brief discussion of the store's history, major accomplishments, and goals.

In addition, new employees need to be trained in the specific tasks outlined in their job descriptions. Although much of their task-specific training will come as they work, they need some specific instruction before they begin. Before beginning task-specific training, ask the following questions:

- What does the employee need to know to complete basic tasks?
- How can I present this information in a manageable form?
- Do the instructions offered accommodate diverse employee learning styles?

After some initial training, be sure to periodically check on the employee's progress and solicit questions about specific procedures.

COMPENSATION

Before determining staff compensation, research what other retailers in your geographic area are paying their employees. To attract and retain good employees, your compensation package (salaries and benefits) needs to be competitive.

Generally, retailers pay sales associates an hourly wage (nonexempt) and management a salary (exempt). However, not all management or salaried employees are actually exempt. Refer to the US Department of Labor website as well as your state and local agencies for more specific information on wages and the rules surrounding exempt versus nonexempt employees. The Federal Fair Labor Standards Act outlines specific characteristics for determining exempt versus nonexempt employment standards.

Consider the following in forming a salary plan:

- Allow for salary ranges for each position.
- Refer to your institutional raise policy for all positions; if none exist, consider raises or bonuses based on merit (tied to your regular staff evaluations) or annual cost-of-living raises.
- Wage differentiation should be based on responsibility and type of work. (Note: Pay close attention to state wage equity laws surrounding how you can apply this differentiation; some states, such as Colorado, have new laws that strictly dictate how to apply this.)
- Benefits are part of the overall compensation package. In addition to standard benefits (health insurance, 401[k], etc.) consider discounts on merchandise, free passes to the museum, or parking privileges.
- For managers or salaried staff, an educational or gift show travel budget may be appropriate.

Salary, benefits, recognition, appreciation, and the opportunity to do interesting, meaningful work are all motivators of good employees.

GOVERNMENT REQUIREMENTS

As referenced earlier, having paid staff requires following federal, state, and local employment laws, which mandate the maintenance of accurate human resource files. Most museums have a human resources department that assumes this responsibility. If yours does not, contact the appropriate state and federal agencies for information about the necessary administrative requirements. The Society for Human Resource Management (www.shrm.org) can also be a great resource.

TRAINING AND MANAGING STAFF

No matter how experienced your new employees are, they need training. As your store prospers and grows, all long-term employees need ongoing training to keep up with new developments in retail and related technology. Be sure that your store's mission statement and core values are emphasized in training.

ONGOING TRAINING

To keep your staff up to date on new developments, implement a few simple procedures:

- Conduct periodic staff meetings to discuss operations and invite speakers on special topics.

- Circulate trade publications and interesting books.
- Send staff to seminars and/or webinars; have them share their findings with other employees.
- When pertinent, use MSA webinars and annual educational conferences.
- Encourage staff to visit other stores.
- Publish a store manual that includes descriptions of procedures, such as operating the cash register.
- Provide chances for cross-departmental learning.
- Provide opportunities for job changes.

PERFORMANCE EVALUATIONS

At least twice a year, you should evaluate the performance of your employees. Such evaluations should be scheduled midyear and near the end of the fiscal year.

Providing ongoing appraisal and feedback throughout the year is key to managing successful employees. Formal evaluations with a written review and specific goals need to occur and be kept as part of the personnel file. Evaluations help employees better understand how to channel energies and direct focus. Negative evaluations should never be a surprise for the employee. Six months into the year, conduct a midyear check-in that is tied to written goals. Ideally, the manager should use every tool available to assist employees in successfully performing their job. It is the manager's responsibility to communicate expectations to the employees and empower them to meet expectations.

Evaluations should be objective and focus on specific goals that were developed by the employer and the employee at the beginning of the cycle. You must cite concrete examples of goals that were achieved and not achieved. Be sure that the goals are aligned with the employee's job description.

The review should be a two-way street. Offer employees an opportunity to discuss their strengths and weaknesses along with suggestions for improvement and general feedback. Employee reviews should evaluate a number of qualities that were defined in the previous performance review.

UNDERPERFORMING EMPLOYEES

It is important that you meet with your HR department to get approval on your process for dealing with underperforming employees and any forms used. State labor laws differ.

- Handling workers who are not performing up to standards is a difficult challenge. Always discuss performance concerns with employees when you first see the problem.
- Be specific about the problem or unacceptable behavior you observed.
- Allow the employee to respond.
- Offer the employee a solution or special training to help the employee do the job.

- Be supportive, but clearly tell the employee that you expect the behavior to improve.
- Make a written note detailing the conversation, including employee's comments and date it took place, and put it in the employee's file.

A calm, systematic approach works best. If the problem occurs again, issue a written warning to the employee:

- Describe what you saw.
- Refer to the previous meeting and include the date of that discussion.
- Indicate that the behavior or attitude has not improved.
- Warn that, if there is another incident within a specified period—for example, within the next thirty days—the employee may be terminated.

Certain procedures must be followed when terminating an employee. When dismissing someone, keep the proceedings dignified. Include in the meeting someone the employee respects and who is on a higher level. Do not include a peer. Focus on the future rather than rehashing incidents that led up to the termination. The museum's HR department will usually handle the formality of employee termination.

EMPLOYEE THEFT

Experts estimate that employee theft accounts for 45 percent of all retail shrinkage. To reduce employee theft,

- establish a zero-tolerance policy toward theft and spell out the repercussions associated with transgressions;
- conduct spot checks to see that employees are following proper security measures;
- account for a "no sale" method of opening the cash drawer;
- track refunds, markdowns, and credit documents,
- require that a manager rings up all employee purchases;
- limit the number of keys available and access to the keys for the store and storage areas; and
- make sure the procedures from the delivery point to the place and time inventory is received into your system are secure.

EXIT INTERVIEWS

Exit interviews often provide valuable information to the museum and the employee. Typically, someone from the museum HR department or senior management will handle this task. To maximize objectivity, the employee's immediate supervisor should not conduct the interview.

RECRUITING AND MANAGING VOLUNTEERS

Volunteers are a valuable resource. Many museums rely on volunteers to staff their sales counters, assist in inventory, and stock the shelves. Volunteer labor is advantageous because it cuts down on salary expenses; however, you must make sure you are adhering to federal and state volunteering laws surrounding this area: this provides the store with willing, eager workers and provides valuable documented hours for the development team to use in getting funding from grants and other sources.

Enlisting volunteers also has drawbacks because they might not be flexible in the hours they will work, might be overly sensitive to critical feedback and might not be willing to assume some of the assigned responsibilities.

Should you choose to use volunteers in your store, it is most important to treat them as you would paid staff in terms of showing your appreciation, adherence to policies, and hiring and firing practices.

RECRUITING VOLUNTEERS

Before recruiting volunteers, consider these questions:

- Will this work be meaningful to the volunteer and useful to the store?
- Will the service justify the time and effort involved in training?
- Will adequate supervisory and support staff be provided?
- Will backup be provided if the volunteer does not come to work?
- Is it likely that the right kind and number of volunteers will be available for this job?

To recruit volunteers,

- publish an appeal for volunteers in your museum's membership newsletter;
- contact civic, social, professional, academic, and senior citizens' groups;
- contact corporate community relations offices and ask for space in their company newsletters (an increasing number of corporations reward employees for volunteerism; discuss this with corporate heads and consider being named to help their staff gain volunteer hours); and
- participate in or be a host of a volunteer fair.

Just as paid staff often enjoy perquisites, you might consider rewarding volunteer service with discounts on merchandise, free passes to the museum, or parking privileges.

If you decide to use volunteers, write a volunteer job description and agreement to ensure that you and the volunteer have compatible expectations. Such an agreement also reinforces the idea that volunteer commitments are as important as professional commitments. You might want to write a separate agreement that asks the volunteer to pledge commitment.

TRAINING VOLUNTEERS

Volunteers should receive the same training you give paid employees. They should become familiar with the store's history, goals, policies, and procedures. And, as do paid employees, volunteers need feedback. Appreciation and recognition are often the only benefits they expect as compensation.

RECOGNITION

To keep valuable volunteers, plan to recognize their contributions. The most effective recognition techniques are personalized and appropriate to the individual. Never forget that they are giving a very valuable asset: time.

In addition to standard recognition techniques, such as pins and plaques, consider the individual and what motivates that person. A profile in the museum newsletter, passes for educational seminars, volunteer brunches, and behind-the-scenes training are some ideas for showing your appreciation to volunteers.

Be attentive to volunteers and encourage paid staff members throughout the museum to afford volunteers the same respect they give paid staff.

DISMISSING VOLUNTEERS

Not all volunteers honor their commitments. Some may fail to report for work consistently or complete volunteer jobs incorrectly. Whenever possible, reassign volunteers to other tasks rather than dismissing them. Occasionally, however, you might have to discharge a volunteer. It is wise to outline grounds for dismissal and revocation of volunteer privileges in the volunteer agreement they sign.

CONSULTANTS

As a museum store manager, you may sometimes need an outside source to achieve a goal or perform a task. A consultant is an individual or firm with a particular skill or area of expertise who is in business to sell those skills. Consultants are paid to accomplish a specific task, typically within a specific period. There are many types of consultants with varying qualifications, and you should take care in the decision-making process to match the right consultant with the task at hand.

There are many advantages to hiring consultants. They can offer proven expertise and an independent, objective viewpoint. Their tasks may include the following:

* Market research
* Economic forecasting

- Organization design
- Public relations/advertising
- Computer equipment selection
- Computer software/POS selection
- Staff training
- Management coaching
- Team building
- Store site selection
- Store design and display
- Strategic planning
- Accounting and financial management
- Legal issues

CONSULTANT VERSUS STAFF

Using consultants can be expensive and time consuming, but consultants can also be extremely valuable. Using a consultant is beneficial in, for example the following situations:

- The skills needed are not available within your organization.
- In-house staff members don't have the time.
- Outside help is needed to define a problem objectively.
- The complexity of a project might be handled more efficiently and cost effectively by a consultant rather than staff members.
- A second opinion is needed on in-house approaches. (A "critique consultant" can evaluate how well you're doing or make a final recommendation in an area in which you and the staff conflict.)

On the other hand, a consultant should not be used in the following cases:

- It is more cost effective to use in-house expertise.
- Your store or museum has recently gone through major changes, and it may not be ready for further changes.
- Hiring a consultant to do work for you involves too much time on your part to gather information and implement projects.

PREPARATION

Once you make the decision to use a consultant, thorough preparation can make optimal use of the consultant's time and expertise and facilitate acceptance of the consultant's recommendations. Determine the objectives of the project and the end results desired. Confer with your staff and other key people who are affected by the project.

It's important to involve the staff. Being secretive or vague may give your employees the wrong impression. They may think that a major store reorganization is taking place and it may change their job responsibilities or leave them without a job at all.

With so many types of consultants in business today, how do you find a qualified one with a proven track record? The best advice is to get recommendations from colleagues. Another source of experts is trade magazines. Publications, such as *Museum Store* magazine, run columns written by experts in the field. Consulting associations may give you suggestions from their membership lists. It is best to use someone who is known to have a track record in the area in which you need help and understands the issues of nonprofit retail.

SELECTION PROCESS

Once you develop a list of several candidates, develop a request for proposal (RFP). This gives each candidate a level playing field and also helps you screen respondents. After receiving responses to your RFP, begin evaluating their responses and choose the most qualified for interviews.

Some components of the RFP can be specific characteristics of the ideal consultant for your project and your organization. Consider the following:

- Applicable experience
- Integrity
- Communication skills
- Industry background
- Fit of image and style with your organization
- Location
- Project goals
- Competitive pricing
- Accountability

Develop a set of questions to ask the candidates. Ask open-ended questions that allow the consultants to speak thoroughly and in depth about themselves and their work history. Be careful not to lead them to the right answer.

Here are some suggested interview points and questions:

- Elaborate on your qualifications and experience.
- How do you plan to gain an understanding of our needs?
- How might you approach this project?
- Tell me about some similar projects you have worked on. What were the results?
- Tell me about some of your successes.
- Tell me about a project that did not go as expected. What went wrong?
- How much time do you estimate this project will entail?
- What type of information will you need to begin this project?
- What other clients are you working for? May I contact them as references?

During the interview, make notes about the candidate's interest level, attitude, concern for your needs, personal chemistry, and trust. This is someone you'll be working with closely. You must be able to trust what you're told and have a comfortable working relationship.

If you're nervous about hiring a consultant alone, involve your supervisor, a board member, or your assistant manager. A second opinion is often helpful in a decision of this caliber.

Each candidate will have sent you a written proposal of the project. The proposal should include a step-by-step description of what the consultant will do, the time span, and the costs. From the proposals, you'll be able to determine how thorough and detail oriented each candidate is, and you'll be able to compare the approaches to the project.

Once you've interviewed all of the candidates, check their references. Get the names of past or current clients from each candidate. Try to track down some of their former clients on your own. That way, you won't interview only those clients that the consultants are sure will praise them. Here are some suggested reference questions:

- How did you like working with the consultant?
- For what type of project were they hired?
- Did you get the result you wanted? Why or why not?
- Did the consultant stay within the budget?
- Did the consultant communicate freely?
- Did the consultant respond to telephone calls and email promptly?
- What are the consultant's strengths and weaknesses?
- Would you use the consultant again?

After all of this research, sometimes a candidate clearly rises to the top of the list. Other times, the decision may not be so easy. Two of the candidates may seem equally qualified or the top candidate may not seem right for the project at hand. A second interview with the competing candidates may solve the conflict as may viewing a report from a similar project each candidate prepared for another client. Choose your candidate and negotiate a contract, determining the costs, time frame, and the work to be performed.

EVALUATION

Evaluating the consultant should be an ongoing process throughout the project. It is wise to set milestone dates for both you and the consultant to evaluate the project and its progress.

Once the project is complete, a formal evaluation is in order. This is the time to sit down with your consultant, tie up any loose ends, and evaluate the results. The meeting should entail a review of the project objectives, the consultant's assessment of the project, your evaluation of the project, an appraisal of the relationship between you and the consultant, and a discussion of any remaining steps. When you submit an amount to be approved for the hiring of a consultant, it is a good practice to make the amount about 10 percent higher than you offer the consultant. Frequently, valid issues arise that neither the consultant nor you could have anticipated, and it is only fair to compensate the consultant to resolve the issues. Business relationships are not only about getting the best deal; they are also about fairness and integrity.

SUMMARY POINTS

- Your employees and volunteers shape the character of your store.
- Staff and volunteers require effective and ongoing training to keep current with new developments in retail and DEAI initiatives.
- Treatment of paid staff and volunteers should be consistent in terms of appreciation, adherence to policies, and hiring/firing practices.
- When working with consultants, good preparation on your part makes optimum use of their time and talent.

7

Creating Great Customer Service

Chapter Highlights

- Customer service training
- Engaging with guests
- Balancing customer care with staff support
- Managing upset guests
- Promoting proactive selling techniques
- Customer theft

The experience your store provides to your customers is a fundamental component of your marketing strategy and as influential as any ad. An old retail adage states that a satisfied customer will tell three people, but a dissatisfied customer will tell ten.

Over the past few years, research has shown that customers value the buying experience and the product equally. It has never been more important to create and maintain a company culture that educates and empowers your staff to effortlessly give each visitor the best experience possible. It is often said that the store extends the visitor's experience in the museum. Make it exceptional.

CUSTOMER SERVICE TRAINING

Courteous training breeds courteous service. One of the first rules of retailing dictates that store staff (paid and volunteer) treat customers the way they themselves are treated. Your staff is much more likely to be courteous and pleasant to customers if you are courteous and pleasant to staff themselve .

The staff needs to be trained in the fine points of customer care. Make sure that your training reinforces courteous behavior. If, after witnessing a clumsy transaction, you need to offer an employee some tips, do so with patience and humor. Never ridicule or humiliate an employee in front of anyone.

Handling customers also requires friendliness, composure, a sincere willingness to help, and familiarity with the merchandise. Share the following guidelines with your employees:

- Remind your staff that people buy because of people; they don't just buy products.
- Stand and make eye contact when talking to customers.
- When customers ask for a special product or section, don't point the way; walk them to the proper area and then ask what more you can do for them.
- Show that the customer is the store's most important asset by stopping whatever you are doing when a customer walks into the store.
- Listen attentively to customers' requests, comments, and complaints.
- Be prepared to answer all reasonable questions about the merchandise and the museum.
- Manage customer expectations. An item may be out of stock. Is there another item that is similar? Do you have a date for a restock?
- Remember that your actions speak louder than words.
- Never judge a customer by their appearance.
- Never discuss other customers or transactions.
- Train staff to efficiently use the POS system to assist customers in quickly locating a book or product, pulling up additional information about the items, or capturing customer information if needed for further contact.
- Conclude every transaction with a sincere thank you and an invitation to come back again.

Nonprofit store staff are more than sales associates or clerks; they are ambassadors for the institution. Their expertise extends beyond product knowledge, including exhaustive knowledge of the museum's collections, features, operations, amenities, events, and more. Visitors may also look to staff for directions and recommendations for restaurants and other nearby attractions.

ENGAGING WITH GUESTS

Museum stores have an advantage over for-profit retailers in that we have a natural topic of conversation: our institution. Rather than a stale greeting, we can engage them in conversation using open-ended questions. Some examples include the following:

- Ask if they have been through the gardens, galleries, or exhibitions yet If the answer is yes, ask what their favorite part was; if not, explain a featur e they shouldn't miss.
- Ask where they are visiting from and what brings them to the area.
- Share interesting information about a product they are looking at.

Good service also requires finesse with phrasing. The following tips r e useful to any employees who work with customers or answer the phone.

- For phone calls, if the store is busy, it is better to take a message and ca a customer back than to juggle the phone and a store customer. Neither will feel they have your attention. It is important to make sure you call back. (If the customer needs to be put on hold, say, "Please hold for a moment. I'll be right with you.")
- Hovering and offering too much help can be as aggravating to a customer as too little, so simply remind customers that you'll be happy to answer any of their questions or assist them in any way.
- An essential component of customer service is an informed staff. Not only should employees be familiar with the museum and its collection, but they should be knowledgeable (or know how to get information about) every product on your shelves.
- In addition to having information on the source and educational signifi-cance of museum-related products, they should be able to answer or find the answer to questions about product limitations, construction, care and maintenance, warranties, and additional selections that might be available.

BALANCING CUSTOMER CARE WITH STAFF SUPPORT

Working a public-facing job can be challenging. To truly provide excellent and genuine customer service, your staff needs to know they are supported and protected in their work environment. This extends to being protected from abuse by the members of the public that they serve every day.

Take into account the diverse presentations of your staff members and the various biases and microaggressions to which frontline workers are vulnerable when working with members of the general public.

To begin, in spite of the old and outdated bias, the customer is *not* always right. Customers are only human, after all, and are subject to the same faults, mistakes, and biases as any other person whether in or outside of your store. The customer is always worthy of respect, however, and within the parameters of your store, you naturally strive to do your best to satisfy your customer's needs.

But it's tremendously valuable to your staff to clarify those instances in which they are allowed to assert themselves to defend against a range of possible wrongdoings that customers commit in retail stores every day: from harassment and sexual abuse to racial microaggressions, from verbal and physical assault to fraud and shoplifting. Creating policies and training your staff in ways that recognize the inherent friction in serving a diverse public build a confident team prepared to take your customer service to the next level.

When building your customer service training and policies, remember that team members face different responses from guests based on a wide range of concepts and beliefs that the guests bring into the museum with them. Customer service is not a one-size-fits-all practice. Consider role playing and training for difficult scenarios, such as guests making unwelcome advances to staff or refusing to comply with museum policies based on some characteristic of the employee enforcing the rules.

Consider the following questions:

- In what ways do your retail staff differ from your average museum guests in age, race, gender presentation, or other demographic features? Keep in mind that people often change their behavior depending on who they're speaking to and may be particularly antagonistic to those they perceive as lower status, and to many retail workers are inherently low status.
- What practices can you put in place as a team to support members who face harassment from members of the public?

  - Having a plan preemptively can go a long way toward curtailing uncomfortable situations and ensuring that your staff have confident reactions to difficult situations when they arise.

- Who are your designated customer service specialists, who step in to handle escalated circumstances? What are the practices and safety guidelines in place for them?
- Do you have a guest code of conduct for your museum and/or an antiharassment policy? In what ways is that communicated to your guests, and what is the expected practice for employees to follow when they see infractions?

Whereas abuses are not the scenarios traditionally planned for in customer service, planning for these experiences will empower your team. A workplace that acknowledges these circumstances and prepares to handle them creates an environment that is safer and more pleasant for employees and visitors alike.

MANAGING UPSET GUESTS

The most common service-related complaints indicate that customers object to service that is either inattentive or excessively attentive. Retail marketing surveys reveal that customers object most strenuously to the following:

- High pressure from store staff
- Indifference from store staff

- Overly attentive and excessively chatty store staff
- Store staff ignorance about products

DEESCALATION TECHNIQUES

No matter how good your staff's service is, you will encounter dissatisfied customers. The effective handling of complaints can diffuse anger and turn an irascible shopper into a loyal customer. A team that is trained to handle difficult situations quickly and with grace will extend a better customer experience and create a more welcoming and inclusive museum experience for all.

The following are some sample steps and principles of deescalation:

- Safety first: Prioritize the safety of yourself, your colleagues, and other customers. If the situation becomes physically threatening, call for security or law enforcement.
- Stay calm and neutral: Keep your tone of voice calm and neutral. Do not raise your voice or engage in arguments.
- Assess the situation: Quickly evaluate the level of aggression and any potential danger.
- Maintain distance: If necessary, maintain a safe distance from the customer to prevent physical harm.
- Listen actively: Let the customer express grievances and concerns. Active listening can help the customer feel heard.
- Acknowledge and empathize: Acknowledge customers' feelings and frustrations without necessarily agreeing with them.
- Use "I" statements: Share your perspective or store policies using "I" statements to avoid sounding accusatory.
- Offer solutions: Propose solutions to address the concerns and involve the customer in the decision-making process. If possible, give the customer choices.
  - If you are unable to accommodate the guest's preferred resolution, offer alternatives. Make sure to manage expectations and avoid offering a solution that you can't deliver to appease the guest in the short term only to frustrate them again at a later point.
  - If associates are not able to make exceptions, they can let the customer know that they aren't authorized to approve what the customer is requesting and offer to get a manager.
- Respect personal space: Ensure that you and the customer maintain personal space and avoid physical contact.
- Request assistance: If the situation does not improve or escalates further, call for security or a manager. Avoid handling severe situations alone.

PRACTICE AND ROLE-PLAY

Conduct role-playing exercises to help staff become more comfortable and confident in handling challenging interactions. Rotate roles to gain different perspectives and insights and include a range of situations, such as customers upset over a product, service, or policy.

It's crucial that staff understand when it's appropriate to continue deescalating and when to seek assistance from security or management.

PROMOTING PROACTIVE SELLING TECHNIQUES

Selling is an integral part of customer service. Typically, most of the customers coming into a museum store don't know exactly what they want to buy. They need your staff's assistance. Museum store retailing is different from regular retailing. Customers are often in a hurry to catch their tour bus, tired from being on their feet when in the exhibits, and saturated with information; usually at least one person in their party is anxious to leave. Assisting them helps to alleviate one or more of these situations and may lead to increased sales. Proactive selling includes the following:

- Acknowledging the customer with a smile, eye contact, and/or a verbal greeting.
- Ascertaining an area of interest and, thus, focusing a customer's attention.
- Suggestive selling of products related to the area(s) of interest.
- Add-on selling that enhances the purchase and increases revenue for the store.

A proven technique for increased sales is to offer customers with three or more items in their hands a basket to make it less awkward to pick up more items. You can also offer to hold their items at the sales desk until they are ready. You never want customers to stop shopping just because their hands are full.

Be prompt and efficient in processing the sale, so visitors and their party can be on their way.

CHILD CUSTOMERS

Children are frequent visitors to museum stores. Many visit the store with schools and tour groups; others come with their parents. Many have their own money to spend and the power to influence how accompanying adults spend theirs. Nonetheless, having children in a museum store requires some special measures.

To avoid damage to products, keep expensive and breakable merchandise out of reach of small children. Instead engage children by placing bins and shelves of inexpensive, durable merchandise they can handle and easily reach. It is inappropriate for staff to discipline any child.

Some schools don't allow store visits for several reasons, including it taking too much time or a lack of equity in spending money among the children. An alternative to losing those sales is sending the teachers a menu of preselected gifts at several price points and having the class order in advance. These packages can be delivered to the bus at the end of their visit and opened on the trip back to school.

Your education or visitor services team will have a schedule of school groups well in advance. You may want to set guidelines for the number of children per chaperone. Be sure to get this message to the teachers prior to their visit so they are prepared. Most education departments have a previsit packet they send to the schools when reservations are made and should include your visiting instructions in their packet.

Tip on inclusive language: Don't assume relationships between children and their accompanying caregivers. Children may visit museums with parents, friends, teachers, nannies, grandparents, siblings, or others. Use "your adult" or "your grownup" in place of "your mom" or "your dad."

MULTIPLE CUSTOMERS

A good way to handle more than one customer at a time involves five key steps:

- Acknowledge the presence of customer B while dealing with customer A.
- Flow from customer A to customer B, suggesting things that will occupy customer A's time while you are working with customer B.
- When you move to help customer B, tell customer A, "I'll be back with you in a moment."
- Pace yourself to give adequate and similar attention to each customer.
- When you return to customer A, thank them for waiting.

CUSTOMER THEFT

Customer theft is the second most common source of retail shrinkage. Following these suggestions can help to limit the problem:

- Make eye contact with the customer. This is the single most effective tool against shoplifting.
- Engage customers in conversation when they enter the store. Good customer service is a powerful deterrent.
- Instruct store staff to stop other tasks when a customer enters the store and greet the customer immediately.
- Staff the store adequately.
- Display especially valuable items in locked cases.

- Keep storage areas locked even during business hours.
- Position register and main sales counters where the staff has a good view of the entire store and all the doors.
- Watch for shoppers who try to avoid staff.
- Don't let a demanding customer distract you from the others.
- If you suspect someone of shoplifting, offer to ring up the items in question. This allows them a graceful out.
- Clearly understand the laws and policies of the museum about taking action against (suspected) shoplifters.

Remember that nothing in the store is worth risking injury to a staff member or customer.

SUMMARY POINTS

- Customers value the buying experience and the product equally.
- Empower store staff with customer service training.
- Selling is an integral part of customer service.

8

Developing Effective Marketing

Chapter Highlights

- Marketing as part of a museum
- DEAI and your museum store's brand
- Promoting your store
- Logos and beyond
- Marketing your online store
- Getting the word out

Marketing is the tool—part science and part art—that will shine a light on the museum store you've carefully crafted. Marketing is a rapidly changing field that works across many methods and channels (such as social and print media) to create awareness, attract customers, and generate revenue.

MARKETING AS PART OF A MUSEUM

In many cases, museum stores may have a small or even no budget for independent advertising. Also, in many institutions, marketing efforts are highly collaborative or even completely executed by the marketing department. A store might find itself with no control over the existing brand language of the larger institution, and it may have to jockey for placement and compete with exhibitions, programs, education, and other areas the museum is spotlighting at any given time. This chapter is able to give some practical, real-world solutions that a museum store can put into action within these structures and limitations.

In actuality, museum stores have a brand and marketing advantage because the museum's identity and collection go a long way toward establishing a strong brand voice in its community. The museum store, unlike an independent retail store, is saved from a large part of the task of building community awareness and defining its mission.

The shop at a natural history museum is expected to appeal to fans of natural history, and prospective visitors immediately have ideas in mind of what they anticipate seeing in the museum store. Working in conjunction with the museum's marketing team can help refine core messaging about a specific organization: the particular flavor and voice of natural history within a given community, for example, or around the strengths of an institution's singular collection: the natural history museum that specializes in seashells and the history of a particular coastal village for one hypothetical example. This creates your niche in the community, in museum stores, and in the retail world as a whole for customers.

DEAI AND YOUR MUSEUM STORE'S BRAND

Your museum store's brand plays a crucial role in reflecting the values and principles of diversity, equity, accessibility, and inclusion (DEAI). DEAI is not a one-time consideration. It's an ongoing commitment. Regularly review your store's offerings and practices to ensure they align with evolving DEAI standards and community expectations. Keep your audience informed of your efforts to improve inclusivity and actively seek feedback to guide your future decisions.

When building a thoughtful museum store brand, keep these points in mind:

- Authenticity and sensitivity: Authenticity is key when it comes to your museum store's association with DEAI. Authenticity means aligning your store's offerings, marketing, and overall brand identity with the principles of diversity and inclusion. This includes being sensitive to the cultural significance of the products you sell. It's essential to ensure that the items you offer do not culturally appropriate and that they genuinely celebrate the diversity and heritage of different communities.
- Telling your story: Your museum store should be an extension of your museum's narrative. It should tell the story of your institution's commitment to DEAI. Make it clear how your store's offerings are curated with diversity and inclusion in mind. Highlight products that showcase the work of underrepresented artists and artisans. Use your store's signage, catalogs, and online presence to communicate this narrative consistently.
- Considering diverse audiences: Your store should cater to a wide range of museum visitors and potential customers. Be mindful of the language

and imagery used in your marketing materials to ensure they are inclusive. Consider the unique needs and interests of different demographics. Stock products that resonate with various age groups, backgrounds, and abilities. Ensure that your store is physically accessible and provide options for online shopping to reach a broader audience.

- Participation in cultural conversations: The products you sell in your museum store can be a means of participating in cultural conversations. Stocking items that engage with current cultural issues, artistic movements, or heritage can influence your store's brand voice. However, be cautious not to exploit or appropriate cultures or causes. Authentic engagement with cultural conversations can strengthen your store's connection to the broader museum community.

PROMOTING YOUR STORE

Everyone who comes into the store is a potential consumer. The objective is to turn customers into consumers who spend money in the museum store. This is called conversion. Promotional efforts are aimed at motivating your visitors to action and shop.

When the customer enters the store, all the factors that affect in-store buying decisions—factors that you control—can be unleashed. But these are all effective only once you've got them in your store.

What do you do to reach out and encourage their visit? Marketing communicates the benefit of your products to an external, paying audience. It extends your store's presence to the community by telling stories about the museum and how your products relate.

Marketing activities include the following:

- Email
- Search engine optimization (SEO) marketing
- Social media
- Short message service (SMS) messages
- Quick-response (QR) codes
- Earned media (through public relations campaigns and media releases)
- Brochures
- Paid advertising (online and print)
- Special events

Two threads should run through all marketing efforts. First you must have a consistent theme that is identifiable with the store. This theme includes using the same name for the store at all times and using a consistent logo, design, color palette, and style in all materials related to the store. Use the strength of your museum and museum store's brand to enhance marketing campaigns and serve to make ads recognizable.

The second thread running through all your marketing efforts should be repetition. The existence of the store should be repeatedly noted through as broad an array of marketing vehicles as possible. The most effective and least expensive application of repetition is for the museum to mention the store in every piece of literature it produces. This repetition can be as basic as mentioning the hours of the store in a print ad for an exhibition or as extensive as periodic features about the store in the material sent to the museum membership.

Before embarking on any marketing effort, you must be comfortable in your knowledge of basic facts about your customers and objectives:

- Who are your visitors/customers? (People!)
- Who do you want as new customers beyond those who visit the museum?
- What do people know about the store?
- What would you like people to know about the store?
- What do your customers buy?
- Who is your competition?

As you plan your marketing effort, remember that marketing should be treated as an investment in increased awareness and sales, not as an expense. As with any investment, you want to see analysis to better determine effectiveness and return on investment. Even if you haven't spent any money, determining how constructive any initiative is will be critical to identifying your return on objective. Virtually all forms of social media have the capability of capturing data for this purpose. This gives you the opportunity to make changes in your approach.

LOGOS AND BEYOND

A museum store is a vital extension of the museum's brand. Beyond logos, your brand identity encompasses a rich tapestry of elements that create a unique and memorable experience for visitors. These elements are often found in your museum's style guide.

Understanding and effectively implementing these aspects is crucial for making your museum store a successful part of the overall institution.

- Visual components: This includes logos, colors, typeface, and materials.
- Tone: Your messaging should reflect the tone of your museum. Whether it's academic, friendly, or inspiring, it should feel like an extension of the museum's voice.
- Identified audience: Who is your core audience? This is the specific group of visitors most likely to be interested in and benefit from your product, service, or message.
- Associations and personality: Consider the associations people have with your museum. Are you considered a place of discovery for everyone? Elite? What gaps is your brand identity trying to bridge?

BRANDING

In chapter 1, we addressed crafting a mission statement. Your mission statement is vital in helping you develop your branding message. Creating your customer value proposition (CVP) will also inform your marketing story.

$$CVP = \text{Identified Customer} + \text{Customer Need} + $$
$$\text{Your Goods \& Services} + \text{Your Mission}$$

This may seem simplistic, but fine-tuning this formula will help you focus on your marketing efforts as well as being an invaluable tool in employee training.

Branding is a marketing principle that refers to the overall image of a product or organization. In the corporate world, brand identity can be the same as a company's corporate identity, as with Coca-Cola for example, or it can focus exclusively on a line of products with the parent company relegated to the background.

An effective brand communicates an identity and often is reflected in a store's name, logo, slogan, sign, and colors. But just as important, a brand communicates a message, such as a promise of quality, reliability, or consistency of products. The Smithsonian's iconic sunburst logo is a familiar element in the museum's branding efforts. The logo resonates with the museum's collection, which includes "everything under the sun" and its educational goal to enlighten.

Experiences and perceptions that customers have when they purchase contribute to—or detract from—the branding efforts of a company or store. Branding can be an effective tool in building customer loyalty and ensuring the perception of value for a store's merchandise, which, in turn, can have a positive effect on pricing. A popular brand identity can generate options for licensing your logo or message to other product developers and distributors. Customers look forward to new exhibitions, events, and product offerings when museums and museum stores work together to build an effective brand identity and fuel customer expectations.

BRANDING BASICS

Many large museums enlist the aid of consultants to create brands, but even a small institution can do a lot to develop its brand identity. Although each museum approaches branding differently, here are a few ideas to get you started on branding your museum store:

- Collaborate with the marketing department (if your museum has one) to ensure that you are clear on your institution's key messages and graphics identity program.
- Invest in the identity by developing merchandise tags, gift wrap, and attractive bags that coordinate with the museum's overall graphic look. You can

incorporate these items into your budget and purchase them over time. (Someday you'll be delighted to see your branded bag reused as a picnic tote in the park.)

- Develop and purchase products that reinforce your institution's key messages. (An inferior Rodin copy might not convey your museum's overall message of quality.)
- Some organizations prefer staff to dress the part and wear logo or licensed merchandise. (This serves as free, wearable advertising.)
- Match your service style to your institution's overall identity. (An institution predicated on quality and education should provide quality, educated service.)

MARKETING YOUR ONLINE STORE

Develop a marketing strategy to drive traffic to your online store. Marketing your online store is very different from enticing customers to your brick-and-mortar store. There you have visitors coming through the doors to see the museum. Social media and SEO will drive customers to your online store, along with ads, search engines, links, and a variety of other sources.

Search engine optimization for a museum store involves optimizing the website's content, meta tags, and backlinks to improve its visibility in search engine results, driving organic (nonpaid) traffic and increasing the chances of online sales. In its simplest form, it is using the search terms people use such as, for example, "educational toys," "Matisse scarf," or "animal sculpture" and using these words in descriptions to begin to show up in customer searches. Search engines often produce thousands of matching sites for a given keyword. Strive to be on the first page and in the first five listings.

Advertise your online store everywhere all the time: through press releases, the museum newsletter, events, on bags, on store receipts, through email, on business cards, on signage, and anywhere else it will be seen. You can also highlight special web sales or even extend Museum Store Sunday specials online.

GETTING THE WORD OUT

EMAIL

Effectively marketing through email is a powerful way for a museum store to engage with customers and promote itself. Here you can send information, such as newsletters, blogs, and sales. Start by building an email list by collecting emails from visitors to the museum, website, or even events. Personalize emails to target specific customer segments, such as members and frequent shoppers.

Make sure to stay up to date on email laws. The CAN-SPAM Act, a law that sets the rules for commercial email, establishes requirements for commercial messages, gives recipients the right to have you stop emailing them, and spells out tough penalties for violations.

SEARCH ENGINE OPTIMIZATION MARKETING

Optimize your website for search engines by using relevant keywords related to your products and museum. SEO can be used on online stores and can also be optimized on content, such as blog posts about museum exhibitions or product spotlights. Ensure that your website, whether used on a computer or mobile phone, loads quickly and has a user-friendly interface.

SOCIAL MEDIA

Social media takes many new forms, but the key to each one is a community of interconnected people. Popular social media sites include Instagram, Snapchat, Facebook, TikTok, and Reddit.

Establish a presence on social media by consistently posting engaging and visually appealing content. This can include product photos, behind-the-scenes glimpses, and updates. Make sure to use appropriate hashtags and geotags to increase your post's chance of being discovered. Interact with your audience, respond to comments, and run advertising campaigns to reach a wider audience.

Social media provides the opportunity for both organic (free) and paid marketing. Use the flexibility of this marketing option to test out inexpensive campaigns, target certain audiences, or try out something new. You can also work with influencers for paid coverage of your museum store, which can bring in new audiences.

SMS MESSAGES

SMS message marketing uses text messages to send updates and promotions to customers who have opted in to the service. Stay up to date on laws governing text message marketing, such as the Telephone Consumer Protection Act (TCPA), to avoid fines.

QR CODES

QR codes can be used on museum brochures, signage, receipts, and displays to link to product pages and promotions or straight to your website. These are best used to direct visitors to specific landing pages that are mobile friendly as they are meant to be scanned with mobile phones.

When using QR codes, make sure to include clear instructions and be sure the code itself is printed clearly.

EARNED MEDIA

Every retail organization should engage in earned media efforts. You should be ready with information and high-quality digital photography of products you would like featured and of your store. Let members of the media know that you've expanded your store, developed your own products, or planned a special event: make your store stand out and noticeable. You might be providing them with newsworthy story ideas and create a lasting media relationship.

MEDIA LIST

Prepare a list of all media contacts in your area. Your list should include the following:

- All local newspapers, including dailies, weeklies, and specialized papers
- Any magazines and e-zines published locally, in particular those with a city or regional focus
- AM and FM radio stations
- Television stations, including public and cable stations
- All online resources that are interested in a story about your store
- Special groups who may have an interest in your store, such as art, science, botanical, and zoological organizations; chambers of commerce; and convention and visitors' bureaus

Next break the master list into two lists: one for media releases and one for public service announcements. It is important to have the names of specific editors and news directors.

Note that media releases offer information on events, people, or products that are newsworthy or of special human interest. Public service announcements generally provide information about charitable events or fund drives.

Your media release list should include the following:

- Newspaper editors and reporters of those sections—most likely arts or business—related to the subject of the release
- Magazine editors: check the publication's masthead/staff box, generally printed on one of the opening pages (if the publication has an arts or business editor, direct the release to either or both; if not, address the release to the editor-in-chief or managing editor)
- Radio news directors
- Television news directors
- Radio, television, and podcast hosts
- Editors of trade publications
- Pertinent websites

The list for public service announcements should include newspaper editors for any related sections and public service directors for radio and television stations.

Remember to update these lists regularly. Newspapers and broadcast stations often have high turnover, and it pays to stay abreast of any changes.

MEDIA RELEASES

Editors and news directors will take your media release more seriously if it adheres to their guidelines, often found on their website:

- Email the release.
- Remember that many writers/outlets will publish your release verbatim, so make it very easy for them to do so.
- Include a release date at the top of the page.
- Include the name, telephone number, and email address of a contact: someone who can handle any related press calls.
- Write a catchy headline that tells what the release is about. Use bold type and a typeface that stands out.
- Keep the release to one page. At the end of the release, type -30- or ### to signal that the release is complete.
- Include the most important facts—who, what, where, when, and how—in the first two paragraphs. Save related and support information for subsequent paragraphs.
- Use a quote from an official source. If the newspaper prints your release or if an announcer reads it over the air, a quote suggests that the reporter conducted an interview. Editors like this personal touch.
- Keep the text objective. Avoid superlatives and editorializing.
- End with a paragraph about your store. Tell the editor or news director that your store is not-for-profit and all the revenue supports your institution's mission.
- Proofread carefully before emailing. Don't rely completely on spellcheck. Spelling and grammatical errors undermine your credibility and the image of the store. In particular, check the spelling of names.
- For print and digital editors, consider including images or videos of an item or individual mentioned in the press release.

Remember that media releases cannot stand alone. You should follow up a media release with a telephone call to heighten the profile of the release and offer to answer questions or clarify any points in the release.

MEDIA INTERVIEWS

Occasionally, a reporter will ask for an interview. Such opportunities provide you with a forum for promoting your merchandise and publicizing your store's educational goals. The following are some tips to keep in mind when granting interviews:

- Know what points (no more than three) you'd like to emphasize and try to reiterate them throughout the interview, tailoring your presentation to the framework of the article or program.

- Keep your responses to the point, especially when talking to radio and television reporters who need short sound bites, but also to newspaper reporters, who will find you easier to quote if you're brief.
- Take your time responding to questions as pauses can be edited out of television interviews.
- Avoid defensiveness by preparing in advance for negative questions; avoid repeating any negative phrases the reporter might use.
- Speak in layman's terms and avoid retail or museum lingo, such as provenance, attribution, accession, and UBIT.
- Don't say anything you don't want aired or printed as everything you say in the presence of a reporter is on the record.
- If you can't answer a question, say so, and tell the reporter you'll research the question and provide an answer later, preferably that day. Follow through.
- Respond to all questions—even the painfully basic ones—with enthusiasm, remembering that it is the interviewer's job to ask all kinds of questions.
- Try to conduct interviews in person as telephone interviews can hamper effective communication.
- Make frequent eye contact with the interviewer.
- Pay special attention to your appearance, facial expressions, and posture so you appear crisp, professional, and friendly.
- Have materials on hand, such as a fact sheet, relevant photos, or a brochure on your museum or store, as the interviewer may wish to refer to these later.

BROCHURES

An informative brochure often serves as an effective and continuing promotion tool. Many institutions produce and distribute brochures. At a minimum, make sure vital store information—location, hours, and types of merchandise—is included on the institutional brochure.

When preparing brochures, be sure to do the following:

- Emphasize the tie-in with the museum.
- Keep the presentation simple.
- Avoid including information that dates the brochure.
- Include the street and web address, hours of the store, and a map.
- Use visuals that reflect either the store's merchandise or its mission.

Distribute brochures to hotels, area chambers of commerce, and convention and visitors' bureaus to attract out-of-town visitors to the museum and the store.

BAG STUFFERS

With nearly every purchase, an announcement of upcoming store and museum events can be stuffed into the bag. The sole purpose of this announcement is to set up a return visit.

PAID ADVERTISING

When planning a paid advertising campaign, work with your marketing department to decide what to advertise and then decide on the best medium to get the most from your advertising dollars. Paid advertising can be expensive and reaches a limited audience. Many museums do not want their store to advertise separately as a destination but are happy to include the store in an ad for the organization. The cost of paid advertising depends on the following:

* The size of the medium's audience or readership
* The size of an ad or length of a commercial message
* Its position or slot within a publication or program
* The technical complications of publishing or producing it

The most expensive advertising is not necessarily the best. A social media ad might do more to reach your intended audience than an ad in a magazine.

Another means of advertising is to band together with other local cultural organizations and share the cost of ads. This increases your audience to include theirs, increases community involvement, and lowers the cost.

It is critical that you get high-resolution images of your products that are clear, well lit, and enticing. If you do not have an in-house photographer, you may have to contract this work out. Make sure to reach out to your vendors who may have the high-quality images needed. Remember, your ads reflect the image of your store and the museum; you want to enhance that image.

Think about what you want your ad to do:

* Sell a particular piece of merchandise?
* Promote an event at the store?
* Create general interest in the store?

Depending on your objective, you may want to feature the following in your ad:

* Popular merchandise: Merchandise that already sells well will draw more people to the store. Once these customers enter the store, you can introduce them to an array of different products. Most consumers are followers and are most comfortable buying what has proven to be popular. Many

repeat customers return because they are assured that popular items, especially for gift giving, will be in stock.

- New products: There is a strong concentration of consumers who want to buy what's new. Featuring new products keeps repeat customers interested and the store's image fresh.
- Exhibition-related items: Advertising products that relate to permanent and temporary exhibitions helps to extend the museum's promotional activity and allows the store to reflect the experience the visitors will have.

Before placing an ad, ask or research for demographic information about the media audience. Match your demographic needs with the reader, viewer, or listener profile. Always tailor your ad to the audience.

Consider the life of the ad. Social media advertising can be adjusted to run for a short period or much longer. Radio and television messages last just a few seconds and must be aired repeatedly to be effective. Magazine ads are often viewed repeatedly over the course of several months.

Depending on the content of your ad and the audience you'd like to reach, consider the following sources:

- Social media
- Search engines
- Video platforms
- Local newspapers
- Local magazines
- Radio programs
- Television programs
- Podcasts
- Programs for concerts, dance performances, and exhibitions
- Outdoor ad space
- In-house publications
- Trade publications
- Chamber of commerce magazines and newsletters

Another form of advertising is sponsorship. In return for sponsoring a radio program or a segment on a special broadcast, your store is mentioned and, thus, linked with the production. If you have the budget for sponsorship, be sure to associate your store with programs of suitable quality and image.

SPECIAL EVENTS

Holding special events in the store has many advantages, including distinguishing your store from others while increasing business. Events can also serve to give back to the community and enhance the museum's mission.

Special events can include the following:

- Book signings
- "How-to" demonstrations
- Readings
- Lectures
- Special discount periods
- Trunk shows with artists and craftspeople
- Tastings
- Product launches
- Classes
- Special exhibit store openings

Museum Store Sunday is a global annual event celebrating museum stores and their mission-related products that play a vital role in helping arts, cultural, and nonprofit attractions educate and thrive. To learn more visit, www.museum storesunday.org.

Special events need to be marketed through the tactics outlined, yet they also serve as a marketing tool for your store. Be sure to collect contact information from those who attend special events for future marketing efforts.

In this chapter, we reference various widely utilized online services to support your marketing efforts. MSA does not endorse any specific company, but given the rapid evolution of technology and social media, we strongly encourage you to conduct your research to determine the most suitable options for your store and institution.

SUMMARY POINTS

- Develop a consistent theme that is identifiable with your store.
- Branding can be an effective tool in building customer loyalty and ensuring the perception of value.
- Provide local media with newsworthy story ideas to promote your store.
- Maintain a database of customer information and contact customers regularly to announce new products, special events, and sales.
- Use the power of social media to tell your story.

Glossary

Accent lighting: Illumination of a specific product or display.

Ambient lighting: A lighting system that illuminates an entire room or store.

Automatic cancellation date: The date a buyer specifies on a purchase order as the latest allowable date for shipment.

Automatic reorder: The reorder (replacement) of high-demand merchandise that occurs automatically when the quantity reaches a predetermined minimum.

Average inventory: The average monthly stock level for any given season. Average inventory equals the opening year's beginning-of-month inventory (BOM) plus total end-of-month-inventory (EOM) divided by thirteen (months).

Backorder: An order or part of an order that the vendor cannot fill on time and must ship when goods become available.

Backup order: Additional merchandise reserved by the manufacturer at the time of the initial order so the buyer can get fast delivery on subsequent orders.

Backup stock (reserve stock): Additional goods available in the warehouse/stock area. Particularly important for bestselling staples.

Barcode: A printed series of lines of varying width, as on a container or product, that can be read by an optical scanner to determine charges for purchases.

Beginning-of-month inventory (BOM): Stock on hand at the start of the month.

Bestsellers: Items in each department or classification that sell the greatest in volume.

Big ticket: Higher price or large merchandise items.

Bill of lading: A document for shipments as evidence of the carrier's receipt of the shipment and as a contract between carrier and shipper. In air shipments, it is known as an airway bill.

Branding: Creating a clear, consistent image of your products, services, or organization in such a way as to favorably influence customer expectations, raise customer awareness, and enhance customer loyalty.

Cash discount: A percentage reduction in the billed cost of goods made in consideration of timely payment within a specified period following the date of invoice.

Cash flow statement: A document by which money may be allocated based on anticipated sales and expenditures within a specific period.

Charge backs: Vendor debits; billings made to vendors because of returned or damaged merchandise, co-op advertising, or other adjustments.

Claim: A charge for merchandise damage that occurred while goods were in transit or the carrier's possession.

Close out: 1. Merchandise offered at a reduced price to encourage rapid sale; often includes items that do not sell well, incomplete items or assortments, or items that are to be discontinued. 2. The act of selling such items.

Collect on delivery or cash on delivery (COD): Requiring payment to be made upon the receipt of merchandise.

Common carrier: Government-sanctioned transportation companies that ship items from any party. Common carriers are required to provide scheduled service via established routes and to publish their rates.

Conditional sales contract: An agreement under which the buyer assumes responsibility and payments. Title is transferred to the buyer only after the buyer meets contract requirements.

Confirmation (of order): A merchandise order on the store's official purchase order form signed by the buyer and seller.

Consignee: The party—or agent representing that party—to whom merchandise is released, delivered, or assigned.

Consignment: A selling arrangement under which the vendor retains title to merchandise until the retailer sells them; unsold items are returned to the vendor.

Consignor: A shipment's originator.

Consolidated delivery service: A private business that delivers goods to retailers for a fee (per package).

Cooperative (co-op) advertising: A practice by which a manufacturer or vendor covers all or part of the retailer's costs for advertising specific products.

Copyright (©): Rights protected by members of the Bern Convention, which includes the United States, the rest of the Americas, and many countries overseas. These rights are given to an originator or an assignee to print, publish, perform, film, or record literary, artistic, or musical material and to authorize others to do the same. Caution: Owning a work does not automatically transfer the rights to the owner. Unless the work has gone into the public domain, the rights are most frequently held by the maker or the maker's estate. Legal advice is required.

Cost: The price the vendor charges the retailer for merchandise.

Cost of goods (COG): Purchase price of goods, including transportation and delivery charges, but generally not cash discounts. Referred to as cost of goods sold (COGS) after selling merchandise.

Credit: Authorization that permits a customer to purchase now and pay later.

Credit balance: State in which credits to an account exceed debits.

Credit limit: The maximum amount of credit allowed to be outstanding.

Credit memorandum (memo): A seller's formal notification granting the buyer a reduction in the amount the buyer owes.

Credit voucher: A company official's authorization to grant the buyer a refund.

Debit memorandum (memo): The buyer's written request for a reduction in the amount owed to the seller.

Design development drawings: Drawings that convey the overall look of the store and include lighting plans, fixtures, and architectural elements.

Distributor: A wholesaler who buys from the manufacturer or importer to resell to the retailer.

Diversity, equity, accessibility, and inclusion (DEAI):

- According to the American Alliance of Museums, DEAI is defined as follows:

  o Diversity is all the ways that people are different and the same at the individual and group levels. Even when people appear the same, they are different. Organizational diversity requires examining and questioning the makeup of a group to ensure that multiple perspectives are represented.

- o Equity is the fair and just treatment of all members of a community. Equity requires commitment to strategic priorities, resources, respect, and civility as well as ongoing action and assessment of progress toward achieving specified goals.
  - o Accessibility is giving equitable access to everyone along the continuum of human ability and experience. Accessibility encompasses the broader meanings of compliance and refers to how organizations make space for the characteristics that each person brings.
  - o Inclusion refers to the intentional, ongoing effort to ensure that diverse individuals fully participate in all aspects of organizational work, including decision-making processes. It also refers to the ways that diverse participants are valued as respected members of an organization and/or community. Whereas a truly "inclusive" group is necessarily diverse, a "diverse" group may or may not be "inclusive."
- Also referred to as IDEA.
- May include belonging (B).

Drayage: Charges for hauling merchandise from one area to another.

Drop ship (direct shipment): Having goods shipped directly to the customer, bypassing the store for delivery.

e-commerce: Sales made through an online store.

End of month (EOM): End-of-month dating: discount counted from the end of the month rather than the invoice date.

End-of-month inventory: The stock level on hand at the end of a given month after adjustments of sales, markdowns, markups, shortages, and purchases.

Free on board or freight on board (FOB): The point at which the buyer pays for transportation charges. If merchandise is made overseas, often the purchasing company only pays the freight charges from the US port, not the original.

Freight bill: A bill prepaid by or for the carrier for charges of merchandise payments.

Freight collect: Buyer is to pay freight when goods arrive. If the terms are FOB, the buyer pays the freight bill and deducts it from the invoice.

Freight prepaid: The seller has paid freight charges in advance at the time of shipment. This does not imply the vendor is responsible for the freight charges. If the buyer is responsible, it means the freight charges are on an invoice.

Gross margin: Percentage of gross profit to sales.

Gross profit: Total sales minus the cost of goods sold.

Guaranteed sale: A security measure to remove the buyer's risk. A signed agreement whereby the buyer may return unsold goods after they have been exposed for sale for a given period.

Homepage: The landing page of a website.

Impulse merchandise: Articles of merchandise purchased by the customer on the spur of the moment without predetermined consideration.

Inventory turnover: A measurement of the rate at which inventory is selling. Specifically, the number of times the average stock is sold and replaced during the fiscal year. Inventory turnover = cost of goods sold ÷ average inventory at cost.

Invoice: An itemized statement from the vendor showing charges for merchandise. It should agree with the packing slip.

Keystone: Double the unit cost.

Landed cost: Total cost of imported merchandise, including purchase price, crating, freight, and insurance to the port of destination. Sometimes includes customs duties and taxes levied on shipment.

Lead time: Length of time that elapses until ordered merchandise is available for sale.

Line: Merchandise or services of a similar, related nature offered by a manufacturer.

List price: A printed price, as on a book or card, is subject to trade and cash discounts; the manufacturer's suggested retail price (MSRP).

Loss leader: An item priced in an ad or a store at substantially less than the competition on which little profit (or a loss) is made to generate traffic.

Manufacturer's representative (rep): Either a salesperson working for a manufacturer or a professional sales firm offering the goods of several manufacturers.

Markdown: A reduction in the retail price of merchandise.

Market: (Noun) 1. A regional location specializing in the sale or manufacture of a certain type of product. 2. The city in which major trade shows occur. 3. The building or merchandise mart in which permanent and/or temporary exhibitions may be seen. 4. The specific date of a trade show. 5. The act of going to another city to purchase goods for your store (that is, "going to market"). 6. The geographic, demographic, or other subdivision of the population considered potential customers (also known as marketing area). (Verb) To offer for sale in such a manner as to appeal to a specific or general audience.

Mark-on: Differences between cost price as billed (before cash discounts) and retail price at which goods are sold (sometimes incorrectly referred to as the markup).

Markup: Upward revision of initial mark-on that results in higher than original selling price. Sometimes confused with mark-on.

Merchandise mix: The various items stocked by a department.

Merchandise plan: 1. A projection of the income from sales and of the supporting stock that can be reasonably expected during a specified period. 2. A description of the merchandise to be carried in a store during a given time.

Merchandising: The special display efforts and selling techniques by which merchandise is presented to prospective customers.

Minimum order: The smallest unit of sales permitted by a manufacturer or wholesaler. This may be in units, dollars (or other currency), or weight.

Net profit: Gross profit minus operating and selling expenses, including salaries, benefits, utility costs, insurance premiums, taxes, depreciation, repairs, and maintenance, marketing, travel, etc.

Net sales: Gross sales minus discounts and returns.

Open account: An account with an unpaid balance. Credit relationship in which the purchaser takes the merchandise and pays the charges on the account on a deferred basis.

Open stock: Items kept on hand in the store and sold in either complete sets or separate pieces, especially used in tabletop items.

Open-to-buy (OTB): Also known as planned purchases. The amount of stock that must be procured to maintain the proper on-hand stock levels.

Packing slip: A list of contents included with a shipment. It generally has no prices printed on it but always has quantity and description.

Perimeter lighting: A lighting system that illuminates wall displays while reinforcing the ambient lighting.

Planned purchases: The amount of merchandise planned for delivery during a given period. The addition of planned purchases to the existing stock should not exceed the planned closing stock for that period.

Point-of-sale system (POS): A software program that allows the computer to track and adjust inventory as sales are made with reporting features for analysis.

Prepay: Payment of all shipping charges by vendor although the purchaser is liable. Charges are billed on the invoice.

Prepricing: Retail prices and barcodes marked on goods before shipping to retailers.

Price lines: Setting selling prices within a classification or department within preestablished ranges (price lines) or a preestablished amount (price points).

Price points: Refers to the dollar or cents amount of a price line.

Product mix: Varieties and sizes of goods comprising the basic stock assortments.

Profit-and-loss statement (P&L): Also called an income statement; a record of the store's income and expenses and the resulting profit and loss.

Promotional stock (promotional goods): Stock of goods offered at unusually attractive prices to obtain volume trade; generally represents special purchases from vendors.

Proprietary merchandise: Unique products developed by your institution and tied specifically to the museum and its collection.

Purchase order: Record of agreement made with a vendor that includes costs, discount terms, and method of shipping. It is a legal contract between the vendor and purchaser.

Quantity discounts: A reduction in the cost of merchandise based on the size of the order.

Rate to sale: The sales quantity in units for a given period.

Request for proposal (RFP): A document that asks vendors to outline their services and provide cost estimates. RFPs also include a description of the services needed.

Reserve stock (backup stock): Merchandise not on the selling floor but available if needed.

Retail selling price: The cost price is marked up by a given factor to cover freight in and retain profit when the product is sold.

Return on inventory/return on investment (ROI): Metric that monitors revenues generated by specific product lines, merchandise categories, or entire inventory.

Routing instructions: Provided by the store, to be attached by the buyer to the purchase order, informing the vendor of routing and shipping instructions (types of transportation by which the store wants the merchandise shipped).

Schematic plans: Drawings that trace traffic flow into and out of the store and map out the areas in which merchandise categories will be displayed.

Screen reader: Software programs that allow blind or visually impaired users to read the text that is displayed on a computer screen with a speech synthesizer or braille display.

Search engine optimization (SEO): Optimizing a website's content, meta tags, and backlinks to improve its visibility in search engine results, driving organic (nonpaid) traffic and increasing the chances of online sales.

Seasonal discount: A special discount to all retailers who place orders for seasonal merchandise in advance of the normal buying period. Also called an "early buy" discount.

Shrinkage: The value of book inventory in excess of actual physical inventory. Includes pilferage, breakage, errors in recordkeeping, and sales incorrectly recorded.

Special order: 1. Order to a vendor that represents an item requested by a store customer but which the store does not typically stock. 2. An order for specially manufactured goods that are not included in the vendor's normal line.

Staple merchandise: Items the average customer expects to be in stock.

Stationery: Paper products, such as cards, posters, and gift wrap; often have a subclass called desk accessories that may include relevant products, such as writing instruments, magnifying glasses, bookends, file holders, etc.

Stock keeping unit (SKU): Identification of merchandise for inventory management.

Stock turnover: An index of speed with which merchandise moves in and out of a store. The number of times during a specific period that average inventory on hand is sold and replaced; sales are divided by average inventory.

Substitution: Item shipped or invoiced by a vendor in lieu of ordered item. Substitution can be color, size, style, price, or other pertinent information.

Target customer: The primary customer to whom a retailer plans to cater.

Terms: The "term" of payment for an order is used on invoices to describe the payment deadline. For example, net30 terms mean that the buyer has thirty calendar days to pay after goods or services have been delivered.

Unrelated business income (UBI): Earned revenue made by a nonprofit determined by the Internal Revenue Service (IRS) to be unrelated to their stated mission. Sample revenue streams may be parking, special event rental, and sales in the museum store of unrelated merchandise. UBI rulings change periodically; the Museum Store Association monitors updates.

Unrelated business income tax (UBIT): The income tax payable to the IRS on earned revenue that is determined by the IRS to be unrelated to a nonprofit's mission.

Vendor: The individual or company from which merchandise is purchased.

Wholesaler: An individual or company that buys merchandise in bulk from importers or manufacturers with the purpose of reselling smaller quantities to retailers. The term wholesale price should not be confused with the term at cost. Cost refers to the price the wholesaler pays; wholesale refers to the cost the retailer pays.

Business Formula List

Net Sales = Gross Sales − Discounts and Returns

COGS (Cost of Goods Sold) = Cost of Merchandise Sold + Freight In

COGS% = COGS ÷ Net Sales × 100

Gross Profit = Net Sales - COGS

Gross Profit Margin (%) = Gross Profit ÷ Gross Sales

Net Profit = Net Sales − Operating Expense

Average Inventory at Cost = BOM (beginning of month) Inventory + EOM (end of month) Inventory ÷ 13 (months)

Inventory Turnover = Net Sales ÷ Average Inventory at Retail

Sales per Visitor ($/V) = Gross Sales ÷ Number of Visitors

Sales per Square Foot ($/f^2) = Net Sales ÷ f^2 Selling Space Including Sales Counter

Capture Rate = Number of Transactions ÷ Number of Visitors

Sales per Transaction = Net Sales ÷ Number of Transactions

GMROII = GM% ÷ Average Inventory at Cost

Index

markdown, 30, 46, 47, 76, 109
market, 109
marketing: bag stuffers, 101; branding, 95–96; brochures, 100; with DEAI and store brand, 92–93; earned media, 97–98; email, 96; logos and, 40, 94–96; media and, 97–100; online store, 96; paid advertising, 101–2; QR codes, 97; retail store, 91–92; SEO, 97; SMS messages, 97; social media, 97; special events, 102–3; store promotion and, 93–94, 96–103
marketplaces, online, 13, 37
mark-on, 110
markup, 12, 18, 33, 34, 47, 110
media, 97–100. See also social media
membership, e-commerce, 25
merchandise: consignment, 38–39; impulse, 55, 109; proprietary, 12, 111; staple, 112
merchandise mix, 31, 38, 110
merchandise plan, 12, 14, 110; book purchasing, 31, 32–33; DEAI and, 30–31; developing, 29–30; inventory, 43–49; licensing, 41–43; margins, 34–35; OTB, 43; product development, 39–41; product resources, 35–39; product selection, 3, 31–32; publishing, 41; retail pricing, 33–34
merchandising, 6, 39, 50, 53, 110; artful presentation and, 61–63; experience retailing and, 61; with high inventory turnover, 44, 45; for maximum impact, 59–63; trends, 35; visual display designs, 60–61
metrics, 15–18
minimum order, 110
mission: budget with DEAI priorities and organizational, 20; metrics versus, 18; statement, 3–4
MSA. See Museum Store Association
MSRP (manufacturer's suggested retail price), 34
museum store. See retail store, museum
Museum Store (magazine), 80
Museum Store Association (MSA), 5, 103; Expo, 35, 39; Resource Library, 13, 20, 22, 39, 43; Retail Industry Report, 6, 10, 15; webinars and educational conferences, 75
music, museum retail store, 58–59

net profit, 12, 13, 19, 49, 110
net sales, 110; COGs sold and, 17; gross margin and, 17–18; historical, 10; inventory turnover and, 17; merchandise plan and, 30; sales per square foot calculated with, 16; sales per transaction and, 17; shrinkage and, 49
nonprofit retail, 1–2, 80

onboarding, personnel policies, 72–73
online marketplace, 13, 37
online store. See e-commerce
online wholesale marketplace, 37
open account, 110
open stock, 110
open-to-buy (OTB), 22, 50, 110; planning worksheet for, 43; using, 43
opportunity cost, 47
orientation, personnel policies, 73
OTB. See open-to-buy
overstocking, 37, 45, 47, 49

packaging options, product development, 41
packing slip, 110
paid advertising, marketing, 101–2
partners, licensing, 42
payment card industry (PCI) compliance, 24
Payment Card Industry Data Security Standard (PCI DSS), 24
payment processing, 25
PCI (payment card industry) compliance, 24
PCI DSS (Payment Card Industry Data Security Standard), 24
PCI Security Standards Council (website), 24
penetration, retail pricing, 34
performance evaluations, staff, 75
perimeter lighting, 110
periodic inventory control, 46

visual display, designing, 60–61
volunteers: dismissing, 78; ethics and best practices, 4; recognition, 78; recruiting, 77–78; training, 78

Web Content Accessibility Guidelines (WCAG), 27
website, e-commerce: custom development, 25; customer service, 27; design factors, 26; ethics and best practices, 5; product selection, 26–27; researching other sites, 26; site operation and maintenance, 27; UX, 23, 25, 26, 28
wholesale, online marketplaces, 37
wholesaler, 33, 113
wisdom, leadership words of, 65–66
worksheet, OTB planning, *43*

About the Museum Store Association

The Museum Store Association (MSA) community advances the nonprofit retail industry and its professionals through advocacy, education, and collaboration. Nonprofit retail professionals and providers turn to MSA to build connections, learn best practices, and conduct business to enhance the success of nonprofit stores and their vendor partners. MSA supports museum stores and vendor affiliates by offering industry publications, virtual and in-person education, access to wholesale vendor expos, leadership development opportunities, networking, and professional resources.